D0172874

SHE WHO

Laughs,

LASTS!

LAUGH-OUT-LOUD STORIES FROM
TODAY'S BEST-KNOWN WOMEN OF FAITH

SHE WHO Laughs, LASTS!

STORIES FROM:

BARBARA JOHNSON	PATSY CLAIRMONT	LIZ CURTIS HIGGS
MARILYN MEBERG	LUCI SWINDOLL	THELMA WELLS
BECKY FREEMAN	SHEILA WALSH	CHONDA PIERCE

and more

COMPILED BY ANN SPANGLER

WOMEN OF FAITH℠

ZondervanPublishingHouse
Grand Rapids, Michigan

A Division of HarperCollinsPublishers

She Who Laughs, Lasts!
Copyright © 2000 by Ann Spangler

Requests for information should be addressed to:

ZondervanPublishingHouse
Grand Rapids, Michigan 49530

Library of Congress Cataloging-in-Publication Data

She who laughs, lasts! : laugh-out-loud stories from today's best-known women of
faith/ compiled by Ann Spangler.
    p. cm.
    Includes bibliographical references.
    ISBN 0-310-22898-0 (pbk.)
    1. Religion—Humor. 2. Conduct of life—Humor. 3. Women—Religious life—
Humor. I. Spangler, Ann.

PN6231.R4 S54 1999
818'.540208—dc21
                                    99-052293
                                           CIP

All Scripture quotations, unless otherwise indicated, are taken from the *Holy Bible: New
International Version*®. NIV®. Copyright © 1973, 1978, 1984 by International Bible
Society. Used by permission of Zondervan Publishing House. All rights reserved.

All rights reserved. No part of this publication may be reproduced, stored in a retrieval
system, or transmitted in any form or by any means—electronic, mechanical, photocopy,
recording, or any other—except for brief quotations in printed reviews, without the prior
permission of the publisher.

Interior design by Korina Kelley

Printed in the United States of America

00 01 02 03 04 05 /❖ DC/ 10 9

CONTENTS

ACKNOWLEDGMENTS

Special thanks to Christine Anderson, whose wonderful sense of humor and carefully honed editorial skills were put to good use sniffing out stories for this book. Christine, you are a superb detective, especially when it comes to ferreting out tales that make us laugh! Thanks to Liz Curtis Higgs, who introduced me to the humor of her delightfully funny friends, Nancy Coey and Hope Mihalap. Thanks to my editors, Sandy Vander Zicht, whose sense of humor acted as a barometer for the stories in the book and whose many helpful suggestions strengthened it, and to Bob Hudson for his careful editing and his words of encouragement.

Thanks also to Steve Arterburn, Mary Graham, and Christie Barnes at Women of Faith for their work behind the scenes, helping hundreds of thousands of women learn to lighten up and enjoy their lives with God. Special thanks to Thelma Wells, Sheila Walsh, Luci Swindoll, Marilyn Meberg, Barbara Johnson, and Patsy Clairmont for putting tears of joy into our eyes week after week at Women of Faith conferences across the nation. They have shown by example that laughter can be faith's best friend.

Thanks also to the publishers and individuals who gave permission to reprint the material that follows.

PREFACE

Over the last several years, books blending humor and faith have been increasingly popular, sometimes establishing themselves on best-seller lists for months at a time. Such books testify to our need to season our lives with laughter, remembering the wisdom of Scripture—that "a merry heart doeth good."

Still, some may wonder whether laughter has much to do with belief. After all, the Bible contains not one reference to Jesus laughing. But neither does the Bible mention Jesus sneezing. Surely we cannot conclude that Jesus was a man in every respect except when it came to sneezing ... or laughing? And is it really so hard to imagine him with his arm around Peter or John, laughing at a story he has just told or heard?

I believe that humor is a gift God has given us to enable us to respond to life creatively. Sometimes it can be one of our most potent weapons in times of difficulty or tragedy, allowing us to practice a kind of "one-upmanship" in which we gain the upper hand over our troubles. Perhaps that's what makes Barbara Johnson's books so appealing. Barbara is able to write about her personal tragedies in a way that reflects her hope rather than her despair. By doing so, she spreads that hope to readers, many of whom feel engulfed by their own troubles. James Thurber, the American humorist, put his finger on this dynamic when he said that "humor is emotional chaos remembered in tranquility."

Between the covers of *She Who Laughs, Lasts!* I have attempted to collect the funniest stories by today's funniest women of faith. Though tastes differ, especially in matters of humor, I hope you will find more than a few stories, quips, and commentaries that will tickle your funny bone and do your soul good, whether life right now seems hard or pleasant. Let God remind you of the funny things that have happened in your own life, the twists and turns that have taken you by surprise and delighted your heart. If you look for opportunities to laugh, you will surely find them. And if you cultivate what some have called "a laugh lifestyle," you will soon discover that "she who laughs, lasts."

'Tis More Blessed to Laugh Than to Frown

For those who love God, laughter isn't optional, it's scriptural.
—Liz Curtis Higgs

If you are not allowed to laugh in heaven, I don't want to go there.
—Martin Luther

A LAUGH A DAY
PUTS WRINKLES
IN THE RIGHT PLACES

−Liz Curtis Higgs

*A*ny woman who can, as the Hebrew declares, "smile, laugh, make merry, celebrate, rejoice, and have no fear" about the future is my kind of role model. The lady described in Proverbs 31 didn't just smile, she snorted. She didn't just giggle, she guffawed. She didn't just snicker, she roared. What a woman!

Society values a sense of humor, consistently ranking it in the top five desirable attributes for an employee or a spouse. Among the Navajo Indians there is a tradition known as "The First Laugh Ceremony." The friend or family member who witnesses the baby's first laugh is given the privilege of throwing a celebration in honor of the occasion, considered to mark the child's entrance into society.

I like George Burns's philosophy: "If I get big laughs, I'm a comedian. If I get little laughs, I'm a humorist. If I get no laughs, I'm a singer." Believe me, when I perform, I have a song ready, just in case!

Of course, to be like our Proverbs woman and smile at the days to come, we need to do more chuckling in the present. Our modern sisters are not doing nearly enough merrymaking, I can tell you that. When I encourage women to laugh more, they tell me in tight-lipped, terse tones, "I'm too busy to laugh. I don't have time to rent a funny video, and even if I did, I don't have time to watch it. I don't have time to buy a funny book, and even if I did, I don't have time to read it. I just don't have time for foolishness!"

That's us, all right. Poor dears, we are missing the big picture, which is that all work and no play makes Jill not only a dull girl but also a sick one. Laughter is good for our hearts, souls, and minds. It costs virtually nothing, yet its therapeutic effect tops many an expensive medicine.

Laughing is the one time we express our true selves, our true nature. There is *no* such thing as "image laughing." You can learn how to walk, stand, sit, eat properly, but when you laugh, you lay all pretense aside and just let go. That's why laughing is so good for you. Anyway, Fred Allen says, "It's bad to suppress laughter. It goes right back down and spreads to your hips."

We know we need to lighten up, but the truth is, we can't survive *without* humor.

As you can tell, I have a soft place in my heart for the good old days of television, of watching Carol Burnett transform herself into a washer woman, of watching Jack Benny fold his arms just so, of hearing Red Skelton, a man who once said, "If I can make people smile, then I have served my purpose for God," end his show by whispering, "God bless." We can still watch Dick Van Dyke fall over the ottoman on late-night reruns, but I miss the variety shows, the live television comedy hours, even the early years of *Saturday Night Live*.

Reinhold Niebuhr, best known for penning "The Serenity Prayer," also wrote, "Humor is a prelude to faith, and laughter is the beginning of prayer." For those who love God, laughter isn't optional, it's scriptural. As we all love to repeat, "A merry heart doeth good like a medicine" (Prov. 17:22 KJV). As a woman who believes in the power of faith and humor, I am heaven bent to bring more laughter into our lives.

Joy shows up in the Bible more than two hundred times, but I wish there were more in there about laughter. After all, we know "Jesus wept" (John 11:35 NKJV). Why not another nice short verse to assure us "Jesus laughed"?

I wonder if the big blast of sound we call laughter today might not have been what the psalmist had in mind when he wrote, "Shout joyfully to the Lord, all the earth" (Ps. 98:4 NKJV). After all, they had other words for singing. And if two million Israelites stood around shouting, "Hooray for God!" at the top of their lungs, somebody had to start laughing sooner or later.

When you are the one people turn to for laughter—the life of the party, the class clown, the raconteur—people expect you to always be "on," to be funny all the time. Even those of us who make people laugh for a living can't live up to that expectation. My first pastor, Bob Russell, tells the story of a man who had fallen into such a deep depression that he finally placed himself in the hands of a therapist.

"I have an unusual prescription for you," the therapist told him. "The circus is in town, and last night I saw the funniest clown there ever was. Thirty minutes of watching the Great Rinaldi, and you'll feel a hundred percent better."

With tears in his eyes, the patient replied, "I am the Great Rinaldi."

I have yet to meet a humorist, a comedian, or a clown who didn't have some deep hurt at the heart of his or her humor. When we laugh at something, we are saying, in essence, "I identify with that!" If someone stood up and described all their blessings, we would be disgusted. When they stand up and share all their faults and foibles, we laugh and love them for it.

Laughter does not mean you are ignoring pain, living in denial, or just not aware of the troubles around you. Solomon said, "Even in laughter the heart may ache" (Prov. 14:13 NIV). For me, laughter is how we take a much-needed break from the heartache, such that when we turn to face it again, it has by some miracle grown smaller in size and intensity, if not disappeared altogether.

An Oklahoma woman wrote, "Laughter was the prescription to help me deal with the unfaithfulness and abandonment by my husband for a woman younger than our two oldest daughters. A laugh a day—a good belly laugh—made me well."

We women need to help each other heal our hurts with laughter. That's really my mission in life, why I speak, why I write. I've watched women who were almost bent over with arthritis laugh until they forgot to hurt. "Look at this!" they call out, waving their arms in the air with glee. "No pain!"

And I've known women who've shared their deepest sorrows with me, how they've lost touch with God and with themselves. Then I watch them, sitting in the audience, tears of joy streaming down their faces. "Are you laughing or crying?" I ask them.

"Yes!" they reply.

A MOUTHFUL
OF LAUGHTER

–Barbara Johnson

At some time in life every woman will ask, "What will keep me young?" Is the secret of youth different for everyone, or is there some universal anti-aging potion?

I heard someone say recently that *laughter* is her drug of choice. Simple as that. Laughter is the language of the young at heart and the antidote to what ails us. No drugstore prescription is required; laughter is available to anyone at any time. Laughter's benefits show on our face, in our body language, and in the spring in our step. So who needs a facelift or crazy diets that don't work?

Did you know that one laugh burns six calories? Laughing is jogging for your insides. It increases heart rate and circulation, stimulates the immune system, and improves the muscle tone of the abdomen. Dr. William Fry of Stanford University says laughing heartily a hundred times a day has the same beneficial effects as ten minutes on a rowing machine.

According to *Psychology Today* magazine, laughter goes hand in hand with creativity too. Researchers found that people with a keen sense of humor have a more creative outlook to problem solving than do somber individuals. Tests also showed those who had listened to a comedy album were able to withstand twenty percent more pain than those tested who were not exposed to humor. Other studies show that companies encouraging employees to bring a sense of humor to work are more profitable than those emphasizing business-as-usual. If these facts are true, we should be laughing on a grand scale in everything we do and using laughter as a barometer of success.

If you want to get to know someone, I say: *Don't bother analyzing the way she talks or what her ambitions and ideals may be. Just watch her laugh.* If I were an employer, I'd hire the person who laughs well. If I were a single woman, I'd marry the man who laughs well. If I were looking for a special friend, I'd search until I met a woman who laughs well.

God gave us this capacity to be tickled way deep down inside. Giggles are as contagious as a viral disease. And y'know what? You don't have to be happy to laugh. You become happy *because* you laugh.

One day when my boys were little I came home from shopping and heard all four of them in the kitchen shrieking with hilarity. They were flicking huge spoonfuls of gooey raspberry Jell-O with bananas against a white wall at the far end of the kitchen and watching it ooze down to the floor.

I walked in and asked nonchalantly, "Where's my spoon?"

Tim promptly grabbed a soup ladle and handed it to me. I loaded it with a glob of goo and fired off. It hit the wall with a giant splat. Hey, this *was* fun! I started to laugh, scooped up another load, and let it fly. My boys joined in, and soon the wall was a red dripping mess. We were laughing hysterically—yes, even two hours later as they finished scrubbing the wall and cleaning up the floor.

Today, I wonder if my two oldest boys are laughing in heaven. I think they must be cooking up all kinds of jokes and games around the throne of God. And as for the rest of us here on earth, I think about how the many hours of laughter we shared with Tim and Steve helped prepare us for their deaths. Laughter is to life what shock absorbers are to automobiles. It won't take the potholes out of the road, but it sure makes the ride smoother.

When the losses of life became unbearable for me, I coped and learned to move on by cultivating a sense of humor. Later, seeing everything in a humorous light became a way of life to dissolve disappointment. It works every time. One day, when I ran into a high school classmate, I realized she had aged so much she didn't even recognize me! (See how humor turns everything around?)

There is nothing like a mouthful of laughter. Get some for yourself and everyone else you know.

Chapter Two
Welcome to Womanhood

From birth to eighteen a girl needs good parents. From eighteen to thirty-five, she needs good looks. From thirty-five to fifty-five, good personality. From fifty-five on, she needs good cash. I'm saving my money.

—Sophie Tucker

Veni, vidi, Visa. (We came, we saw, we went shopping.)

—Jan Barett

CROSS MY HEART

—Liz Curtis Higgs

*S*haron had one. Judy had one. Even Mary Ann had one, for crying out loud, and everybody could see she didn't need one yet.

Okay. I didn't need one either, but after that first gym class in seventh grade, it was clear the time had come.

I simply had to have a bra.

Some mothers made a big deal out of buying this particular foundational garment for their daughters. Judy's mom presented it to her in a pretty pink box filled with fluffy tissue paper and a special card: "Now that you're growing up . . ."

Mary Ann got a matching slip and panties with hers, in bright solid magenta. She couldn't wear a white blouse for weeks.

Sharon and her mother went to the store together to pick hers out. It was a special "trainer" model, AA, no batteries included, but it definitely gave her power. She was "in."

And I was "out." I was still underdeveloped enough for undershirts, but those went out of style with waist-high undies. Of course, I was still wearing those too, but that wasn't the problem. The problem was the top half.

I casually mentioned buying a bra to Mother one day, who promptly "tsk-tsked" and assured me, "When you really need one, we'll buy you one." A quick check in the mirror told me the need level was low. Flat didn't even describe the situation. Concave was closer to the truth.

Secretly, I toyed with the idea of visiting Charlotte's Dress Shop on Main Street and buying one myself. *Could I get away with it? Would Mom find out?* I wondered.

One afternoon on the way home from school, after yet another humiliating "no show" in the locker room, I sneaked up the concrete steps and through the door into Charlotte's. The bell above the door tinkled loudly. I licked my dry lips as I prepared to ask a clerk the dreaded question, "Where are your ... foundations?"

Thank goodness, there they were on full display. Not like the nylons Mother bought me that came in little flat boxes stacked floor to ceiling behind the counter. No, these mysterious wonders were each in their own box with a see-thru window. Apparently, you simply picked one out, marched to the counter, plunked down your money—no problem!

Wait. Big problem: 32A? 34B? 36C? What in the world did those mean? I was an A-minus student ... did I need an A-minus bra? As I peered at the confusing array, I sensed someone moving toward me and spun around to find Charlotte herself, grinning knowingly, tape measure in hand.

"Were you looking for a particular size, dear?"

Gulp.

"Slip your jacket off, and let's see what we need, shall we?"

We needed a 32. Actually, we needed a 28, but they didn't make one. She measured at the full part too.

Twenty-eight inches. (For the record, my waist was also a 28.) Then Charlotte chose the most promising box from the top corner of the rack and pulled out the undergarment. An embarrassing blush started creeping up my neck and around my ears as she directed me toward the dressing room. When she'd check on me in a few minutes, she'd know the truth. I didn't need a bra at all.

I think she noticed but didn't say a word. "How does it feel?"

It felt like heaven. I smiled in the mirror, imagining my very own Playtex marvel making its debut at my next gym class. Never mind that the cups looked like empty pockets. I was finally going to be "in."

"I think this will do, don't you?" Charlotte purred, heading for the register. "That'll be $7.95 plus tax. Shall I charge it on your mother's account?"

"No!" I almost shouted, then blinked back tears. *$7.95! I had no idea!* "No thanks, I'll just . . . uh, come back for it tomorrow."

Undershirts were $2.50, tops. I had $4.00 to my name. Who could have imagined such an exorbitant price for something so . . . small? I dragged myself home, more discouraged than ever. No way was I bringing this up with Mom again. I would have to find another solution.

That solution was waiting for me in the trash can. My sister, Mary, nine years my senior, had tossed out an old bra that had lost its zip. No question, it would take some effort to turn a 34B into a 28AAA, but I was desperate. Firing up our sewing machine, I stitched the cups as flat as I could make them, added new seams to each side, and adjusted the shoulder straps.

Ta-da! It looked awful and felt worse, but if I moved fast in the locker room, no one would notice. I washed it by hand so Mother would never be the wiser and hid it in my closet to dry.

The next day in gym class, my pathetic excuse for a bra was nonetheless greeted with junior high enthusiasm—they even wrote a cheer to celebrate, along the lines of "Give me a B! Give me an R! Give me an A!" I was delirious.

Got away with it too, for nearly a week, until I carelessly tossed my makeshift bra in the laundry hamper Friday afternoon. By the time I remembered, Mom had gathered up the clothes and headed for the laundry room. I was toast for certain.

Mom never said a word. Not Saturday, not Sunday. I was in agony all weekend. Monday morning, I found a plain white box on the top of the laundry basket. Yikes! *Mary's recycled bra with a stern note?*

I lifted the lid, grateful no one was watching my hands as they shook. "Oh my!" I said aloud, my spirits lifting instantly. It was a brand-new, lace-trimmed, ribbon-sporting brassiere, better than anything Charlotte had to offer. Perfect for a young lady in training.

A voice from the doorway brought up my head with a snap. "I realized it was time," Mom said, smiling slightly, watching me with something like regret in her eyes. "Welcome to womanhood, honey."

I didn't trust myself to speak, so instead I pressed my cheek against hers and squeezed my eyes tight enough to hold back the tears. Finally, I managed to whisper, "Thanks, Mom."

My mother almost never laughed out loud. This time, she laughed out loud. "Don't thank me for that, daughter dear! Believe me, the novelty will wear off soon enough."

As usual, Mom was right.

TECHNO-WONDERS
OF THE MODERN AGE

–Sue Buchanan

*P*salm 139, verse fourteen says, "I praise you because I am fearfully and wonderfully made; your works are wonderful, I know that full well."

"Fearfully made?" Yep, and if I doubt it, all I have to do is look in the mirror first thing in the morning. A scary sight! There's a hymn that says, "Look ye saints, the sight is glorious." Hmm, not in my mirror! At least not before Maybelline!

Not too many of us sit around and think about the fact that we are wonderfully made. In fact, quite the opposite is true. We complain about our bodies continually—that we're too fat, or our hips are too big, or our breasts are too small, or they sag.

Mine will never sag! After breast cancer I had reconstructive surgery, so even after everything else goes to pot, my techno-breasts will remain perfect. Someday they'll dig up my body—decayed beyond recognition—and there they'll be, still pointing heavenward! In my case, the verse could read, " . . . fearfully and artificially made."

Not long after I had my overhaul (so to speak) and was still feeling very body-conscious, I had an important meeting. It not only included several representatives from the company I was producing for but several suppliers as well. I wasn't just on the spot to come up with workable ideas, but I was in charge of leading the meeting and responsible to negotiate a win-win situation for everyone.

That morning I dressed carefully. I put on my new electric-blue pants suit Wayne had gotten me in Chicago—my very fashionable and, in my opinion, quite stunning electric-blue pants suit—the drama of which was in the draping effect of the neckline. It could be worn two ways depending on the mood. You could wear it with a blouse or camisole and leave the neck open; or you could wear it (I thought) without a blouse and pull the draping to one shoulder and attach it to a large, asymmetrical button. This particular morning I made the without-the-blouse choice.

The meeting went well at first, but somewhere along the way the negotiations with one of the vendors broke down. We simply couldn't come to an agreement. At last, in frustration (and for effect), I stood to my feet, smacked the table with my palm, put my hands on my hips, and said, "I'm sorry. This just isn't working for me."

Wow! My theatrics seemed to be working better than I'd hoped. Everyone came to attention like a precision drill team; shoulders straightened, chins dropped, and mouths flew open. Then, just as I was mentally patting myself on the back for being so savvy in my leadership skills, all eyes (eyes that seemed to be popping out of their sockets, I might add) shifted from my face to my chest. My eyes followed their gaze; when I saw what they saw, I thought I would die right then and there. One whole side of me— albeit covered in a black lace bra and draped in electric blue—had popped out for the world to see.

The room got so quiet you could have heard an ant breathing. Finally, one of the men broke the silence. He turned to the others, put on the silly face he knew would get the laugh he was after, and said, "Well, it sure is working for me."

In Ephesians 2:10 it says, "We are God's workmanship." Another translation uses the word "masterpiece." I certainly wasn't thinking about being God's masterpiece that memorable day. I laughed with the others, but I must say I was more than slightly embarrassed.

But think about it! I'm a masterpiece! You're a masterpiece! Isn't that another reason for us to compliment each other—even be lavish with our praise? After all, we are praising God when we do that. And if others say good things about us and we twist and turn, uneasy while being complimented, well duh! We are denying our Father his just worship.

When someone says, "You are God's child; you are beautiful; you are talented; you are a true gift to my life!"—just say thank you!

THE MAMMOGRAM

—Barbara Johnson

*A*s mothers and wives, we spend many years with our children, teaching and preparing them for life—specifically, preparing them for school, friends, and social graces—and with husbands, who start as mavericks until we train them to become thoroughbreds. But with all the time and energy we expend teaching our family these things, no one is standing in the wings to instruct *us* about anything. No one prepares us for the situations that come in our lives. *No one!*

Recently a friend sent me this bit about *how to prepare for a mammogram!* Since then I have shared it in conferences and listened to the uproar of laughter—sharing this has boomeranged back to me the most overwhelming hilarity. So this is just my boomerang of fun to you. As you share this, you too will enjoy the genuine boomerang principle; as you make another one laugh, you yourself will enjoy the laughter!

The Mammogram

This is an X-ray that has its own name because no one wants to actually *say* the word "breast." Mammograms require your breasts to do gymnastics. If you have extremely agile breasts, you should do fine. Most breasts, however, pretty much hang around doing nothing in particular, so they are woefully unprepared. But you can prepare for a mammogram right at home using these simple exercises.

Exercise 1: Refrigerate two bookends overnight. Lay one of your breasts (either will do) between the two bookends and *smash* the bookends together as hard as you can. Repeat this three times daily.

Exercise 2: Locate a pasta maker or old wringer washer. Feed the breast into the machine and start cranking. Repeat twice daily.

Exercise 3 *(advanced only please)*: Situate yourself comfortably on your side on the garage floor. Place one of your breasts snugly behind the rear tire of the family van. When you give the signal, have your hubby slowly ease the car into reverse. Hold for five seconds. Repeat on the other side.

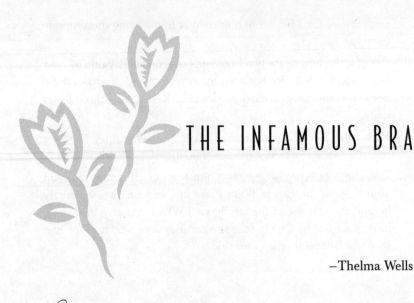

THE INFAMOUS BRA

—Thelma Wells

Ladies come to the Women of Faith conferences with all kinds of issues and situations. And a few of them seem to be a little over-the-top: You know, their compass seems to be headed in the opposite direction from the rest of the world.

That's the impression TJ gave at a conference attended by fifteen thousand women earlier this year. While other women were applauding the singers and speakers, TJ waved a white, size 44D, lace brassiere in the air, as high as she could.

She had come with a busload of ladies from her church, but some of these fellow travelers were embarrassed by her unusual interaction with those on the stage. Her pastor's wife vowed to take that thing away from TJ. But she wasn't giving it up easily. Instead of handing over the bra, she swirled it in the air and yelled, "Hallelujah," at the top of her voice. All her parish pals could do was act as if they didn't know her.

I met TJ when she ran up to my book table during a break with the big bra in hand and enthusiastically insisted, "Sign my bra! Please sign my bra! I want you to sign it right here!"

I looked at her in shock. I have signed T-shirts, books, audio-cassette and CD covers, brochures, programs, bumblebee pin cards, earring holders, postcards, and tablecloths. But bras, never.

I thought, *If TJ has the nerve to sling a bra around in front of thousands of women and then ask me to autograph it, that's the least I can do.* I signed it, "My cup runneth over!"

That autographing moment was the beginning of a wonderful relationship that has included spiritual growth and renewal for me. When I returned home from the conference, TJ telephoned and asked me to speak at her church for Multicultural Celebration Day. She said she had attended the Women of Faith conference asking God to direct her to the person the Lord wanted as speaker for the celebration day. She was convinced God had led her to ask me.

The theme for the daylong celebration TJ organized was "Fresh oil—a new and fresh anointing uniting the body of Christ." And the day truly was a time of reconciliation for the body of Christ in that Methodist church in Arkansas. Along with learning to sing "What a Friend We Have in Jesus" in Japanese, we were enlightened, encouraged, and inspired by representatives from Scotland, Russia, Puerto Rico, Mexico, Germany, Switzerland, Israel, Spain, Romania, Bulgaria, Korea, Poland, as well as Native Americans and African Americans.

As the keynote speaker, I explained that every culture represented there had roots stemming from the flood survivors—Mr. and Mrs. Noah, Mr. and Mrs. Shem, Mr. and Mrs. Japheth, and Mr. and Mrs. Ham. But the most powerful time was after I spoke and the charge for reconciliation was given by TJ. We all sang, "Let there be peace on earth, and let it begin with me," as we went to each other with love, hugging and holding each other and saying words of apology or comfort. At that moment, all of us seemed to realize that we are sisters and brothers, valuable members of the human race regardless of origin or ethnic background.

Sharing communion was a beautiful sight. All the cultures represented were around the altar, tearing pieces off a loaf of bread and dipping into the same cup of wine.

Just think, if I hadn't signed that infamous bra, I might have missed the opportunity to participate in the most prayed-up, planned-up, and thought-out day of cultural togetherness of my life. And I learned that not all people who act a little over-the-top should be labeled "offsides" just because they do things differently from the norm.

Have you missed the opportunity of a lifetime because you thought the person who offered it was the sort who would use a size 44D bra as a flag? I'm not suggesting you throw caution to the wind. But I am suggesting that if someone presents you with an unusual opportunity, check your gut feeling before you write it off. God gave us intuition that can work for us when we let it. I don't suggest waving a brassiere at a conference, however. Leave that for TJ.

I WAS A VICTIM
OF TSK-TSK-ERS

—Sue Buchanan

*I'*d quit speaking publicly tomorrow if it weren't for the fact that I love the opportunity it provides to travel around the country and collect new "old friends." If the truth be known, I can't wait to finish speaking so I can talk one-on-one; it never ceases to amaze me how strongly you can bond with a person even though you have only a few minutes together. Whether it's a word of affirmation, a joke, a prayer request, or a life story in a nutshell, I feel privileged to share a few private moments with these friends.

The theme of my message (and I use the term loosely) is that I spent a lot of years thinking I had to change my whole persona in order to make God happy with me. I thought he couldn't possibly want a wacky, offbeat—even shallow—person like me representing his interests. But surprise! Surprise! He does! And surprise! Surprise again! Half the people I meet are every bit as wacky and offbeat and shallow as I am. "After hearing you speak, . . ." they say, followed by a huge pause that hangs in the air like cigar smoke at a poker game. (Now there's a perfect example of not knowing what I might say next—I've never in my life played poker, at least not while smoking a cigar.) "After hearing you speak, . . ." they say. *Eeeeeeek!* I'm thinking, *here it comes!* I'm bracing myself! "I've decided, I'm just like you. I'm crazy!" *Oh, you poor soul!* But here's

33

the clincher; here's what makes it all worthwhile: "It never dawned on me before that it's okay to be crazy—okay for me to be *me*—that I can be crazy and still be God's person." *Wow! It took me years to learn that.*

Sadly, many women (and men too) I meet are managing to mask their very spirit so they'll feel accepted by their church friends. After speaking in California recently I received a letter from one of my new "old friends," June.

"I've read your book *I'm Alive & the Doctor's Dead,* and I'm delighted with your sense of humor," she wrote. "I have one too but I have to watch where I use it. Today in our Bible study the question was asked, 'What does it mean to stand fast?' I said, 'It means to stand up in a hurry.' No one laughed or even thought it was funny." If I'd been there, I would have fallen off the chair laughing, and June and I would have been thrown out of the Bible study on our derrieres.

At a church conference in Florida, a cute little lady, who claimed to be in her seventies, came up to me and commented on my rather (okay, *very*) short skirt and very high-heeled shoes. "I'm just like you," she said, "I have great legs." (That was a new one.) With that she pulled her dress up to her undies and did a pirouette. Sure enough, her legs were as shapely as any Radio City Music Hall Rockette.

"I've been covering up these legs with long, dreary"—she named her church denomination, one known to have a lot to say about *adornment*—"skirts all my life. But today I'm gonna go out and buy me a dress that will show off my best feature—my legs."

Another time, a gray-haired woman, also claiming to be in her seventies, stood on one foot and then the other till I finished signing books. She then pulled me into a corner and, with a look that suggested she might be going to ask my help in overthrowing the government, whispered, "You're a prankster; I can tell you're a prankster. I'm just like you; I'm a prankster too!" She winked a conspiratorial wink.

"I want to tell you what I pulled on my husband," she said. "You'll love it, and you can do it to your husband when you get home." By this time, she's giggling and blushing, and I'm wondering what in the world she's going to say.

"I came in from shopping the other day and my husband said, 'What did you buy?' I said, 'I bought a two-piece red outfit. You're gonna love it!' He said, 'Well, try it on; I want to see it.'" She gave a wicked little snicker. "I can't believe I'm telling you this, but I went in the bedroom, took off all my clothes and put on red knee socks. I went prancing out right in front of him. He almost had a heart attack."

I'll admit I was shocked out of my mind; this woman had "pillar of the church" written all over her! "I strutted around all over the place," she said, "and he just loved it. He still has a good laugh every time he thinks about it." Then she took hold of my arm and whispered, "I'd never tell my church friends that, they'd die; but I can tell you 'cause you're a prankster. Go home and try it. Your husband will just love it." (I know what you are wondering, and my answer is "none of your business.")

It makes me sad to think there are women in their seventies who have spent a lifetime of energy holding back instead of letting go. And it's probably because years ago someone pronounced a disapproving "tsk-tsk" and it became a curse on their lives. Maybe it wasn't an audible click of the tongue, perhaps it was a wag of the finger or a disparaging "look" to put them in their place—and they've been stuck in that "place" for fifty years. It makes me so sad to think about this that I'm crying as I write—I was there!—I was a victim of tsk-tsk-ers!

Don't wait until you're seventy to give yourself permission to be who God made you. Go on! Get out there! Let down your hair while you still have some! Relax and let yourself be the wacky, wild, wonderful woman you really are!

Chapter Three

Did I Do That?

He is mad past recovery, but yet he has lucid intervals.
—Miguel de Cervantes, *Don Quixote*

Sometimes one likes foolish people for their folly, better than wise people for their wisdom.
—Elizabeth Gaskell

LOOKIN' GOOD

−Patsy Clairmont

$\mathcal{I}$ remember the day well. It was one of those times when everything goes right. I took a shower and fixed my hair. It went just the way I wanted it to, as it so seldom does. I pulled on my new pink sweater, giving me added color, since I need all the help I could get. I pulled on my gray slacks and my taupe heels.

I checked the mirror and thought, *Lookin' good!*

Since it was a cool Michigan day, I slipped on my gray trench coat with pink on the lapels. I was color coded from head to toe.

When I arrived in downtown Brighton, where I intended to take care of some errands, I was surprised to find heavy traffic. Brighton is a small town, but it has a large health food store. Usually I can park right in front and run in.

But today business was so brisk I had to park two blocks away. When your attitude is right, and it's a great day, however, inconveniences and interruptions are no big deal.

I thought, *I'll just bounce down the street in time to the sunshine.*

I got out of the car, bounced down the street, crossed the road, and entered the store.

As I headed toward the back of the store, I caught my reflection in the glass doors of the refrigeration system. It reaffirmed I was lookin' good. While enjoying my mirrored self, I noticed something was following me. I turned and realized it was my pantyhose!

I remembered the night before when I had done a little Wonder Woman act and taken pantyhose and slacks off in one fell swoop. This morning I put on new panty hose and must have pushed the old hose through when I pulled on my slacks.

I believe they made their emergence as I bounced down the street in time to the sunshine. I remembered the truck driver who stopped his truck to let me cross. As I looked up, he was laughing, and I thought, *Oh, look! the whole world is happy today.*

So I waved. Little did I realize how much I was waving.

I assumed I had reached some amount of maturity by this time in my life, but I can honestly say that when I looked back and saw that ... that ... dangling participle, the thought that crossed my mind was *I am going to die!*

I knew they were my pantyhose because the right foot was securely wrapped around my right ankle. I knew it was secure because I tried to shake the thing off and pretend I had picked it up in the street.

It's amazing to me that we gals buy these things in flat little packages, we wear them once, and they grow. Now I had a mammoth handful of pantyhose and no place to pitch them. The shelves were crowded with groceries, and my purse was too small and full, so I stuffed them in my coat pocket. They became a protruding hump on my right hip.

I decided to never leave that store. I knew all the store owners in town, and I figured that by now they would have all their employees at the windows waiting for a return parade.

I glanced cautiously around the store and noticed it was Senior Citizens' Day. They were having their blood pressures read, so I got in line to avoid having to leave the store.

The bad news was no one noticed I didn't belong in line. The good news was I had an elevated blood pressure reading. Usually nurses take mine and say, "I'm sorry but you died two days ago." Today I registered well up the scale.

Finally, I realized I'd have to leave. I slipped out the door, down the street, into my car, and off for home.

All the way home I said, "I'll never tell anyone I did this, I'll never tell anyone I did this, I'LL NEVER TELL ANYONE I DID THIS!"

I made it home and got out of the car. My husband was in the yard, raking.

I screamed, "Do you know what I did?!"

He was so proud to know his wife had gone through town dragging her underwear. I told him I thought we should move—to another state—in the night. He thought that was extreme and suggested instead that for a while I could walk ten feet behind him. After thinking that through, we decided it should be ten feet in front of him so he could check me out.

If you have ever done anything to embarrass yourself, you know that the more you try not to think about it, the more it comes to you in living color. As I walked through my house, the replay of what I did came to me again and again.

At last I cried out to the Lord, "You take ashes and create beauty, but can you do anything with pantyhose?"

Almost immediately I realized that I had dragged a lot worse things through my life than pantyhose. I dragged guilt, anger, fear, and shame. I was reminded by the Lord that those were far more unattractive and distracting than my hose, for they prevented others from seeing his presence and his power in my life. I needed to resolve the pain in my past that I might live more fully today and look forward to my tomorrows.

Excuse me, but what is that you're dragging?

IN THE PINK

−Liz Curtis Higgs

*I*t's not that I don't adore home decorating. That love affair began at the dawn of puberty when I turned twelve and my two older sisters had vacated our big bedroom. Mother decided I was old enough to choose a new decorating scheme myself. Did I do a safe pale blue, a feminine pink, a slightly daring lavender? No, I went for a Mother Nature look: navy blue walls (think sky) with bright yellow floral wallpaper on the ceiling (sun), brown painted floors (dirt) with green throw rugs (grass, of course). And to think Earth Day hadn't even happened yet. I was ahead of my time. Way ahead of my time.

Mother, being a gardener, thought it was dandy. She even helped me antique the desk and bookshelf−remember that look? We used yellow paint for the base color then brushed on dark blue stain and wiped half of it off. It looked as bad as it sounds: green and yellow striped furniture. My friends made gagging sounds when they walked in the room.

I've traveled the interior design highway many times since then. My first apartment furniture consisted of one metal pole shelf earned with S&H Green Stamps and a dreadful plaid sofa bed bought with a credit card. Next came the early seventies hippie look with oversized floor pillows in earthtone colors: tans, browns, and rust. (Did we really decorate with olive and orange?) When it came to decorating, I found my best bet was paint. It was inexpensive, came in a zillion colors, and required no sewing, stuffing, or hauling. There wasn't any shade I wasn't willing to try: dark green, paper bag brown, turquoise, even feldspar.

Feldspar? The dictionary will tell you it's something found in igneous rocks, but I'm telling you this is *not* a color found in nature. Picture the deepest, brightest coral imaginable, then multiply it by ten. That's feldspar: a color one should use in very small doses, which is why it seemed the perfect choice for my tiny six-by-seven-foot laundry room.

Never one to rush such projects, I waited until the night before the delivery men would arrive with my new washer and dryer to start painting. How long could one little room take? Anyway, the hardware store insisted it would cover in one coat. I popped open the can and gasped. Feldspar my foot, this was flamingo pink! With trepidation, I poured it into the paint tray and was soon rolling it onto the walls.

Flat and vertical, the color was more coral than pink, and I sighed with relief as I rolled and trimmed, rolled and trimmed. By 1:30 A.M., I had finished three walls and was pleased with the progress, except for one minor point: it was going to take two full coats to cover the old paint. Filling up the paint tray for the last wall, my tired arms stretched the tray up onto the shelf that perched on the side of the ladder.

Maybe it was the late hour, the lack of sleep, or too many paint fumes, but my next move was a terrible one: I moved the ladder. The forgotten paint tray, filled with a quarter of a gallon of bright pink latex, came raining down on my horrified head. If my mouth had been hanging open as usual, I might have drowned. Instead, the metal paint tray landed right on my chest, cascaded paint down the front of my T-shirt and jeans, and landed with a clang at my feet.

Now, the good news: for the first time in my natural life, I had used a drop cloth. On previous painting expeditions, I'd taken one page of newspaper and scooted it around the room with my foot, painting as I went. But because this laundry had a nice hardwood floor, I had wisely covered it with a vinyl drop cloth, a fact that at that moment gave me great solace. It could have been worse.

Had I been a married woman then, I would've called out, "Honey!" and some kind man would've come to my rescue. But I was a single woman when I bought that house, and the only other creature under my roof was my large cat, now perched on the laundry doorstep, looking mighty curious.

I know what most of us would've done: we would've stopped right then and there and gotten ourselves all cleaned up before continuing. But I was not about to waste all that paint, and anyway I had a job to finish. So, I stepped up to the fourth wall and smeared myself all over it, trying to make use of every drop of feldspar on my body. By this point, the clothes were a write-off, so I wiggled out of them, turned them inside out and dropped them in the trash can. (I know what you're thinking: does she always do her decorating projects in the buff? No, but when you live alone, you can get away with a lot!)

It was now 2:00 A.M., the first coat was complete and would have to dry for two hours before the second coat could be applied. Certainly at this point a sane woman would have taken a moment to jump in the shower and wash off all that pink paint, but it seemed so pointless. In two hours, I'd be back into the mess all over again, I reasoned, so I simply pulled back the comforter on my bed, pulled back the sheets, pulled back the mattress pad, and positioned myself on top of the mattress. The paint had only landed on my front half, remember, and it was completely dry by now, to boot.

I set the alarm for 4:00 A.M. and immediately fell into a deep sleep. Two hours later, I woke up on the first ring, rolled and trimmed with feldspar abandon, then showered and dressed for the day and was drinking coffee at 8:00 A.M. when the delivery men showed up at my door, appliances in tow. Despite my late-night latex disaster, I was going to have a lovely laundry after all.

But later that morning, driving to work, a terrible thought came to mind: what if I had died in my sleep? After all when you're single, weeks can go by before anyone notices you're not around. I could imagine my coworkers finally beginning to ask, "Has anyone seen Liz this month?" until at last the police would break into my house and find a stiff, half-naked pink woman with a starving cat perched at the foot of her bed. Gives me the willies to think about it. Ever since then, my color choices have been more subdued, a favorite being Heirloom Beige, which matches my aging skin perfectly.

OVERCOMING WITH WORMS

–Becky Freeman

*M*any authors these days have a symbol of their own unique personality. When we think of Barbara Johnson, we visualize geraniums in broad-rimmed hats. When *Worms in My Tea* appeared in bookstores, I never dreamed my name would be forever intertwined with a slimy invertebrate.

While touring my publishing company for the first time, an eager young woman introduced me to a group of salespeople by proudly announcing, "This is Becky Freeman—she's our author with *Worms*." (Don't you know how eager they were to shake hands with me after that intro?) Since that happened, I've played around with the idea of changing my business card to read:

Becky Freeman
"The Author with *Worms*."

Or better yet, I've thought about using the name *Worms* as an acronym for my own organization.

WORMS, INC.
Women Overcoming Ridiculous, Mind-boggling Situations ©.

To assume the leadership of such a prestigious organization as WORMS, INC., one must, of course, have the necessary qualifications and experience. Besides the volumes I've already written, I'd like to submit the following story as proof of my credentials.

One Thanksgiving our family was visiting Scott's parents, who live about two hours driving distance from us. Scott and the children decided to stay over for an extra day, but I needed to get back home to work on a writing assignment. So I drove home alone, leaving late that evening. On the drive home, I went the wrong direction several times because it was dark, and, well, you know how different the world looks when the lights are off.

When I finally arrived at the gate to the entrance of our little lakeside community, it was around 2:00 A.M., and I found myself in the first of a series of mind-boggling predicaments. I hadn't remembered to get a key to the gate from Scott. I contemplated turning away and driving to a motel but thought, *No, that would be silly. Our house is only a mile down the road there beyond this locked gate.* So I parked on the side of the road, took my keys and my purse, locked the doors to my car, and walked up to the seven-foot gate. Tossing my purse over the top, I waited until I heard it land with a thud on the other side, then I began my ascent over the gate.

A middle-aged woman doesn't get many chances to climb fences, and I actually thought it was rather fun. Like being in the third grade again. Of course, I'd rather have enjoyed this jaunty climb on a sunny day, rather than on a cold, misty night at 2:00 A.M—but we overcomers must look on the bright side, mustn't we? I picked up my purse from the asphalt, resolutely slinging it over my shoulder, and began the mile-long trek to our home. Have I mentioned how dark it was yet? I felt like Snow White walking through cartoon shadowy forests, the trees taking on a dark life of their own on either side of the road. The hoot owls once made me jump with such a sudden start that I dropped my purse and had to grope for it on the ground like a blind woman.

I kept repeating comforting verses I'd learned as a child: "At times I am afraid I will trust in Thee," "You are a very present help in times of trouble." Before long my heart stopped pounding, and I was actually beginning to enjoy the quiet night and the stars overhead. Until my new boots rubbed two fresh blisters into the sides of my tender feet. I was also beginning to feel the painful effects of having downed a supersized cola on the drive home.

Finally, thankfully, I made my way to my front door and nearly fell on the welcoming front porch with gratitude. "Ah, home sweet home," I said, leaning against the door to open it. But something was awry with my home sweet home. The door was locked. Now, I realize that for most people this is not unusual. Most folks lock the front doors of their houses when they go away for any length of time. But since we were only gone for the day and Scott knew I'd be coming home alone, a locked door raised all sorts of dire suspicions. Then I realized something else: the dogs weren't barking. Daisy, our Brittany spaniel, and Colonel, the little schnauzer, *always* bark either in greeting to us or in warning to strangers. Something was terribly wrong with this picture, besides the fact that the door was locked, and I was once again, keyless (not to mention, clueless).

Burglars, obviously, had killed the dogs and locked me out of my own house. I hate it when that happens. But "we shall overcome" is my motto, so I did not give up. I would go find help.

Where does one go for help, however, on foot, at 3:35 A.M.? My feet bleeding, my head pounding, I grabbed up my purse and marched toward our neighbors, Melissa and Michael Gantt. *Yes!* I brightened when I saw their car in the driveway, *At least they are in town.* I hated to wake them up at this hour, but I felt, for my own safety, that I had to get someone to help me find a way into my house and who'd provide comfort if I should need to grieve the loss of my pets and all worldly possessions.

I knocked and knocked. And knocked and knocked. Not a creature would stir in my neighbor's house. I turned the knob, and to my surprise the front door popped open. "Melissa!" I yelled. Nothing. "Michael!" I hollered. Still all was quiet. *Great,* I thought, *maybe the burglar got Michael and Melissa too.* So I walked into the darkened kitchen, noticed a phone with glowing buttons, picked it up, and called Scott's parents' home.

"Beverly?"

"Yes?"

"I'm so sorry for calling this late. Or this early. I guess it's morning, isn't it? Can I please speak to Scott? I've broken into my neighbors' house, and I'm using their phone because I can't break into our house."

"What?"

"It's a long story. Could I just speak with Scott?"

"Sure," she answered, and in few seconds Scott was on the phone.

"Becky?" he asked sleepily.

"Yes?"

"Why am I talking to you on the phone at four in the morning?"

"Well, Scott, . . .," and I explained what had happened up to that point. "So you see," I continued, "I'm worried because the doors are locked, and the dogs are probably dead. And I'm in someone else's house without their knowledge, using their phone to talk to you. And they may be dead too, but I'm too afraid to go look and see."

"Don't you dare, Becky," Scott said quickly. "You are lucky Michael hasn't woken up and shot you thinking you are an intruder."

"I *am* an intruder, just a friendly one."

"But they don't know that!"

"What should I do?" I lowered my voice to a whisper.

"Go home. I locked the doors this morning and forgot to tell you. The dogs are probably over at George's house down the street. You know how they love to go over there when we're gone—he's always feeding them treats and letting them in for a visit."

"How will I get in?"

"Climb through the side window."

"Gotcha. See ya tomorrow—if I'm alive and all."

"You'll be fine."

I gently put the phone down, wondered if I should risk using the Gantts' restroom before I left, decided my bladder would have to tough it out, and tiptoed back out of the front door, forcing my aching feet back to my home. I had to get a ladder to reach the unlocked window, but once inside, I nearly kissed the linoleum. The dogs were nowhere to be seen, and the house was completely ransacked—exactly as we had left it. I breathed a sigh of relief, ran to the bathroom to take care of my most pressing need, then took a hot bath, put Band-Aids on my blisters, and fell into bed. *All is well,* I thought as I finally fell into a deep slumber. *Only you, Lord, make me dwell in safety. Thank you for taking care of me. Together, we have overcome.*

I'd been asleep a full hour before the phone rang. I checked the red digital numbers on the alarm clock: 5:30 A.M. Picking up the phone, I wearily answered, "Hello?"

"Becky?" the voice on the other end sounded concerned.

"Yes?"

"This is Janet—I live near the gate."

"Yes, Janet, what's up?"

"Well, I'm sorry to call so early but the paperboy came by this morning and gave me a credit card belonging to you. Said he found it on the ground near the gate."

I explained what had transpired the night before, and Janet offered to pick me up, take me to the gate, and open it with her key. I accepted her offer—this way I could also get my car off the road and check for any more credit cards that might have fallen out of my purse when I threw it over the gate. When I got to the gate, sure enough I found another credit card sticking out of a pile of leaves. I thanked Janet for her help and told her to pass on my gratitude to the paperboy, then drove back home.

You know, I'd better check my purse to see if there are any more cards missing, I thought before I dropped back in bed. But now, my purse was nowhere to be found. I looked everywhere I could have possibly left it. "I can't believe this!" I yelled aloud to an empty house. Then I realized what probably happened. *I must have left my purse outside the window when I crawled in the house. A burglar must have seen it there in the porch light and stolen it!*

I dialed the sheriff's office. It was now 6:15 A.M., and I'd had more activity all night long than I get in most days. When the dispatcher picked up the phone, I said, "Yes, this is Becky Freeman. I just wanted to report a stolen purse, in case you recover any of my checks or credit cards or anything."

"And where was your purse stolen?"

"It was stolen where I left it outside last night when I crawled through the window to get into my house." I explained as best I could what had transpired during the night and my theory on my purse's disappearance. The dispatcher seemed anxious to get off the phone but wished me the best in locating the purse snatcher.

I'd better call the Village Market too, I thought. *It's the closest place for a burglar to try to pull something like that.* Michael and Melissa are not only our neighbors and friends, they also own the Village Market. Melissa answered the phone.

"Hello, Gantt's Village Market, can I help you?"

"Melissa?"

"Becky?"

"Melissa! You're not dead!"

"No," she sounded confused, "but I feel like it. I had to open the store this morning, and Michael and I had both taken antihistamines last night for our colds. I'm still having a hard time keeping my eyes open. Becky?"

"Yes?"

"The weirdest thing happened—we found your purse in our kitchen this morning."

I was so embarrassed. After I explained my breaking and entering to Melissa, I called back the sheriff's department.

"Please don't worry any more about my missing purse," I explained jubilantly. "I found it! I left it in the other house I broke into last night! Isn't that wonderful?"

The dispatcher agreed that it was and quickly hung up the phone.

Relieved to have located my purse, and exhausted, I fell back into bed and into a deep sleep—for an entire thirty minutes—before the phone rang again at 7:00 A.M., still a mite early to be getting calls on a weekend morning. I picked up the phone and recognized the sweet voice of another friend and neighbor, Wally. "Becky?" There was something oddly familiar about the way this conversation was starting.

"Yes?"

"Becky, I was jogging this morning and about halfway between the gate and your house, I found three of your credit cards!"

"Oh, Wally, thank you! I must have dropped them out of my purse when that owl hooted." Then I went through the entire story again with Wally, who sounded even more confused by the time I'd finished. I had to admit, the saga was getting more complicated with every phone call. The next day, my son found the last missing credit card on the road while riding his bike. Apparently, I'd been like Gretel of fairy-tale fame in those wee morning hours, only instead of dropping crumbs I'd been dropping credit cards to mark my path.

I am so blessed to have friends and neighbors who are honest and caring, the kind who understand when you break into their house and leave your purse, but you don't know it so you have to call the sheriff and report it stolen, and then, when you find out it wasn't, have to call back and retract the report. Friends supportive of my struggle to be a WORM: a woman overcoming yet another string of ridiculous, mind-boggling situations.

So, WORMS of the world, wriggle out to the porch and relax. Not only is there now a support group for us, but we can hold our heads up out of the dirt with pride as we realize anew our purpose on earth: to give the rest of the world a chance to pause, scratch their heads and ask, "What?"

KEEP
ON TICKING

—Bodie Thoene

*W*hen I first went to work as a writer in the motion picture industry years ago, I had no idea what a Rolex was. I confused it with a Rolodex, the desktop file secretaries use for addresses.

I was mystified when the battery of my Timex died and I had to ask the secretary how long it was until lunch.

"Hold on," she said, "I'll look at my Rolex."

Suffice it to say, I was the only living human being on the West Coast over the age of three who did not know what a Rolex was. Eventually I figured out *what* it was, but it took Emma, the secretary, to explain *why* a Rolex was such a big deal.

"Handmade," she explained. "I mean, everything is *handmade!* Once the jeweler sets the thing, it is set forever! It even adjusts the days for leap year! Can you believe it?"

"Big deal," I replied. "Is it so hard to change the date on your watch for leap year?"

Emma's eyes narrowed. She had saved the best for last: "I personally know this guy who lost his Rolex out on the ocean over the great Marianas Gorge! No one knows how deep this gorge is or what is down there, right?" She paused for effect. "So this guy accidentally drops his $2,000 watch into the water over the gorge. His wife is yelling that he should go after it because she bought it for him for their anniversary. But this guy does not love her enough to jump into the Marianas Gorge after a watch—no matter what! But then two years later, what do you think happens?"

"I'm listening."

"They catch a great white shark right off Catalina Island, and what do you think they find in its stomach?"

"Not the husband. He didn't jump."

"They found . . . the Rolex!" She raised her hand scout's honor. "With his name engraved on it!"

"Bet he was glad he wasn't attached to it."

Emma would not be stopped. "But listen to this!" She grabbed my arm, and I could see she had goose bumps. "The Rolex was still ticking! Imagine! Dropped into the Marianas Gorge. Who knows how deep? The pressure! Then to be swallowed by a great white shark! Who knows how much that poor Rolex went through—and still survived!"

I had to admit, there were some Jonah-like qualities to the story that made me eye the watch with a new respect. It was no wonder the entire writing staff of ABC television owned Rolex watches. This way they would never miss a deadline, even if they were swallowed by a shark in the Marianas Gorge. I was the only writer with an excuse.

After that, I admit, I wanted a Rolex too. But the years passed, and I never got my Rolex. Then last year a dear friend returned from a trip to the Orient and presented me with a red velvet watch case. To my astonishment, inside the case was a *Rolex watch!*

Like a character in a Porky Pig cartoon, I stuttered something unintelligible: "Such a gift! So incredible! How did you manage to do it?"

My friend began to laugh. "It's not a real Rolex, silly! I've been to Taiwan, not Switzerland! I bought it off an eight year old with an armful of the things!"

I tried not to look disappointed. It was the thought, after all. She had been thinking of her materialistic friend back in the States who in a million years would not purchase herself a real Rolex.

"Gee," I said. "It sure looks real."

The only visible difference between a Rolex and its counterfeit was the way the second hand moved. The real Rolex simply swept across the dial while the counterfeit Rolex said, "Tick. Tick. Tick." Every other detail was the same.

Okay, I know it's shocking, but I admit it: I wore the watch. I wore my sleeve rolled up when I wore the watch.

I was very careful to take it off around water. Washing dishes, brushing teeth—all these sorts of things were done without the watch. Things went well. I stayed away from the Marianas Gorge.

But one day I found myself in line with my teenagers for Splash Mountain at Disneyland. My kids were all around me saying things like, "Ah, Mom! Come on! Don't be a pansy! You won't get wet!"

I had been having such a good time that I forgot about my Rolex. Signs on the wall of the ride warned off people with heart trouble and bad backs. Everywhere I looked were stenciled words that proclaimed: CAUTION! YOU MAY GET WET!

My heart and back were fine, but I worried about my white blouse. My kids said, "We'll block the water! You won't get wet!"

They are my beloved children, after all, so I believed them. I climbed into the little Splash Mountain log. I screamed and laughed around every curve. I was not getting wet. And then, when the last loooooong hill down took us into the water, my beloved children ducked while the full wave splashed over me.

My soaking wet white blouse was remedied when I quickly put on my son's sweatshirt. But there was no help for the fake Rolex. Before my very eyes, its crystal fogged until I could no longer see what time it was, much less its counterfeit trademark.

There has to be a moral to this story, right?

I tacked the phony Rolex onto my corkboard, then took my old Timex down to be cleaned. And no longer do I wonder, with the lyrics to a recent song, "Would Jesus Wear a Rolex?" Instead, I wonder, *What kind of watch would he make? And if I were a watch, what sort of watch would I want to be?*

I know I want the trademark of his craftsmanship stamped on my face; no counterfeit faith for me. Confronted with *real* tests, I want the promise of his presence: "If I take the wings of the morning, and dwell in the uttermost parts of the sea; even there shall thy hand lead me, and thy right hand shall hold me" (Ps. 139:9–10 KJV).

Simply put, I want to keep ticking—even in the great Marianas Gorge!

NIGHT LIFE

−Patsy Clairmont

*W*hen my parents called in the middle of the night because their furnace broke, Les went to help them. I felt a little pang of discomfort at being left alone. Well, to say I was alone isn't accurate—both our young boys were upstairs asleep. Also, our fearless cockapoo, Tuesday, was snoozing outside.

Tuesday was a lovable dog, but she had no discernment. She greeted beggar and thief, as well as doctor and chief, with sloppy enthusiasm.

She also had what I thought was a strange defect for a dog. Her barker was broken. Seldom if ever did she *gr-r-r* or *arf.* That was until . . . The Night of the Broken Furnace.

Les was gone about an hour when the barking began. I was startled at the unfamiliar sound and thought it must be a stray. I peeked out cautiously. Tuesday was on our porch, arfing in the direction of the woods. Oh, yes, did I mention we were living on a Boy Scout reservation containing six hundred acres of woods, swamps, lakes, and assorted monsters? The latter was my immediate concern.

Stop and think about it. What else would cause a bow-wow's broken barker to suddenly kick in?

Tuesday began to run from the front door to the back door to the front again. I knew what this meant. Whatever was out there was closing in.

I crept out of bed and began to look for a weapon. I had always believed investing in the Kirby vacuum cleaner would one day pay off. This was the day.

I took the long nozzled tube section to bed with me for protection. I placed the telephone beside me with the phone book open to emergency numbers. My heart was thumping as I strained to hear sounds of the approaching monster.

With Kirby in hand, I rotated my vision from watching the window to the door, to the window to the door, when suddenly I turned my head too far and caught my reflection in the mirror.

You want to talk about frightening ... no ... make that ridiculous.

I said to myself, "What's wrong with this picture?"

I've known the Lord well enough and long enough to realize he wants to be my refuge and hiding place. Here I was, trying in my anemic strength to handle this imagined invasion.

I laid down my Kirby sword and picked up the sword of the Spirit, which is the Word of God. I reviewed every peace and power promise I'd ever read. I'm not sure how long I'd been reading when fear started to drain out and quietness began to seep in, and I nodded off.

Soon I was sound asleep. I never heard my husband when he pulled up in front. I didn't hear him when he came in the door. I didn't even hear him when he entered our room. I didn't hear him until he shook my foot and asked, "What's the vacuum cleaner doing in bed with you?"

Men and Marriage–What Could Be Funnier?

Nobody will ever win the battle of the sexes. There's too much fraternizing with the enemy.

–Henry A. Kissinger

We cannot really love anybody with whom we cannot laugh.

–Agnes Repplier

[In marriage:] Sometimes we submit; sometimes we outwit.

–Ruth Bell Graham

HANKY
PANKY

—Charlene Ann Baumbich

*G*eorge and I were engaged in lively conversation when he stopped talking for a moment and retrieved his white, no-frills hanky out of his back pocket. Unfolding it, he vigorously blew his nose. I continued to talk without skipping a beat.

After several good snorts, he folded the hanky right on the creases, again and again, until it was returned to its perfect square. He put it in his right hand and slid it down into his back pocket.

When he looked up at me, I had become mute. My mouth was agape. I couldn't believe what I was seeing, and it showed on my face.

"Is something wrong?"

"Do you always fold your hanky like that after you blow your nose?"

"Yes. Is that a problem?"

"Maybe."

"Why?"

"After twenty-five years of married life, I had no idea you folded your hanky back up like that after blowing your nose."

"So?"

"So, I'm sorry to tell you that when I'm doing laundry and find the hanky so neatly folded in your back pocket, I assume it hasn't been used and I simply put it back in your drawer without washing it."

It was George's turn to stand with his mouth agape. After a couple beats passed, he responded.

"No wonder I always have so much trouble getting my glasses clean."

APHRODISIACS

—Betty Smartt Carter

*M*y husband and I are private people. Never, ever would I discuss our sex life in public—offering up the most sacred, intimate moments of our marriage to be examined by strangers.

So why don't I tell you about my good friend—um—Judy, instead? Okay. Judy and Bob have always had a great relationship. It used to drive everyone crazy, how crazy they were for each other. They held hands, smooched loudly, talked baby talk. When Judy and Bob walked into a room, the temperature shot up about ten degrees; mold started to form on bread. In their first year as husband and wife, they sanctified the marriage bed at least once a day. They often dashed home from church to drink water from their own cistern before company arrived for dinner.

In some ways, the years have only improved things. Judy and Bob still get along great, and they're still very passionate. But even the happiest couples have differences, and on one intimate subject, Judy and Bob have always disagreed. Bedwear.

Judy started married life with a drawerful of bridal-gift negligees. Like so many wedding presents, they didn't exactly suit the bride's taste. The only other time in her life Judy had worn red satin, for instance, was to her sixth-grade Halloween party, when she dressed up as the Human Torch.

Mysteriously, though, Bob seemed quite pleased not only with the red satin camisole but also the black fishnet teddy and the leopard-spotted thing (whatever it was).

This worried Judy. Bob had never shown such bad taste before! They had experienced a wonderful, almost mystical level of agreement on everything from carpet swatches to cubism. From what dark depths of his soul had sprung this passion for man-made fabrics and loud colors?

Judy went along with it as long as the wedding presents lasted. She wore the red camisole till its spaghetti straps had turned into vermicelli. She wore the leopard-spotted thing till snaps shot off the underside with a loud "ka-pop!" Then, when the last of the tasteless nighties had been trucked off to Goodwill, Judy breathed a sigh of relief and wore what she liked to bed. Most of the time, a T-shirt.

See, for Judy, what's sexiest is what's most comfortable. Bob's old T-shirt was as sexy as it got—soft, see-through (after years of heavy use), and easily removable. No snaps to fly off at awkward moments. No straps to get hooked on the bedpost by accident. No scratchy lace to cut off her circulation.

Bob seemed to think the T-shirt was temporary. "You going to wear a T-shirt to bed again, Honey?"

"Is something wrong with that?" Judy asked.

"Well, it's okay some of the time, I guess, but it's not very sexy."

"You're wearing a T-shirt, Bob. I think you're sexy."

"That's different. All I'm saying is a little variety is nice."

The next night the weather cooled down a little, so Judy hauled out her old navy-blue-and-green flannel pajamas with lace around the high collar. They looked like hand-me-downs from Eleanor Roosevelt.

"You said you wanted variety!" she declared when Bob winced.

"That's not what I had in mind."

"Bob, this is what *Victoria* really wore to bed."

He sighed. "No wonder she kept it a secret."

Judy didn't stop wearing her T-shirt. She had a right to be comfortable, she thought. But then she put herself in Bob's shoes. On any given day at work he saw how many pretty, well-dressed women? Thirty? Forty? Stopping for gas on the way home he often passed racks of porn magazines, their lurid covers only half-disguised in peekaboo brown paper. Back on the road he headed past a sign for Hooters: "Made You Look." The world had it in for godly, married men like Bob. Deliciously packaged, faultless female bodies littered his life, yet he was supposed to hurry home to the woman in the Florida Gators T-shirt? Maybe it was asking too much.

Resolved to do her husband a favor, Judy headed to the lingerie store, taking a friend along for emotional support. The negligees they examined fell into two categories: pretty pastel cotton things that she liked and slinky cartoonish numbers that would probably appeal to Bob.

"Moo," said Judy, holding up a nightie that wouldn't fit Gwyneth Paltrow on a diet. "I give up. Let's go home."

"Judy!" her friend snapped. "Remember? You're doing this for Bob."

In the end, Judy marched up to the cash register and plopped down a hot-pink negligee with the brand name "Breezy Love" printed on the tag in the back. "'Sleazy Love' is more like it," she mumbled, pulling out her checkbook.

"Come on, Judy," her friend coaxed. "It's not like you're going to be wearing it all night!"

That night, Bob smiled when he pulled back the covers. "Hey, what happened to the T-shirt?"

"I gave it the night off," she said.

"Makes me feel kind of sorry for the Gators."

"Not to worry. They'll be back on the old gridiron tomorrow."

PART MAN, PART BARCA-LOUNGER

–Sue Buchanan

*P*roverbs says, "He who finds a wife finds what is good and receives favor from the Lord." No offense, Lord, but that may not always be true. I've known several cases where a man found a wife, and it was a bad thing–very bad thing! There have been stories in the news about wives doing dreadful things to their husbands.

Even in our own case (though I've never been known to do bodily harm, as has been the case in some of the news articles), there have been times Wayne has questioned whether finding a wife was such a good thing. One of those times might be when he wants to watch a ballgame on TV *for the millionth time* and I don't want him to.

From a wife's perspective, "watching a game" is synonymous with "sleeping through a game," and sleeping includes snoring, groaning, drooling, and twitching. Wives understand that even though the viewer is asleep, the television must be turned up to the highest possible decibel of sound. And we know, having learned our lesson the hard way, that if you turn the TV down or off during said game, the viewer wakes up and acts as though the Lord has returned and he's missed it–and it's your fault!

I'll admit I'm high-maintenance and need a lot of attention, and I know it can't be fun and games all the time–even playing

Twister in your underwear can get old if you do it every night! But another ballgame? Puh-leeze! I've heard that Elvis Presley was known to pull out a gun and riddle the TV screen with bullets. Let me put it this way: *it's a good thing I don't carry a gun!*

I do have my secret ways, however, to punish Wayne—whoops, make that *tease* Wayne—and entertain myself on game nights, which with cable seems to be every night of the week.

Dizzy, our yellow cat, loves to stretch out on Wayne's leg and wrap her little paws around his thigh as he watches TV. After both are asleep, I've discovered that if I talk to Dizzy, in a certain tone of voice, it makes her so happy she'll "make bread" with her paws and dig into Wayne's leg with her claws.

"Dizzy, you're a pretty little cat," I say, and her paws start moving. Wayne winces! I wait a little while and begin again. "Dizzy, Dizzy, look at you, such a sweet kitty." She digs! Wayne winces and jerks! "Dizzy, you're such a happy kitty. Such happy little paws." Wayne is practically in spasms, but he doesn't wake up. Sometimes this goes on for a very long time. Sometimes it's my entertainment for the entire evening. Sometimes Wayne wakes up and makes popcorn.

Sometimes, dear God, I'm as mean as a snake! Help me! Amen.

FINISHED YET?

–Sheila Walsh

$\mathcal{B}$eing stretched for money for any length of time can do funny things to people. My friend Phil was a staff evangelist for Youth for Christ. Like all of us who worked in the ministry, he must have sometimes wondered how he could possibly make ends meet. Our need kept us on our knees most of the time.

One night Phil and his wife splurged on a steak dinner at a nice restaurant. While they were enjoying a lovely meal, Phil noticed that the man seated opposite them was leaving after only picking at his T-bone steak.

"More than three-quarters of that steak is left," Phil said indignantly. "What a waste!"

"Never mind what he's doing," his wife replied. "Enjoy your meal."

"But that's a huge piece of steak, and it'll go to waste," Phil continued. "They'll throw it out."

A few minutes passed, and then he said, "I'm sorry, but I just can't allow that to happen."

As he stood up, his wife hissed, "Sit down! What are you going to do?"

"Stop worrying," he whispered. With that he sneaked over to the table, wrapped the large piece of meat in his napkin, and then slipped back into his seat.

"What did you do that for?" she asked in disbelief. "What are you going to do with it?"

"I'll give it to the dog," he said, a satisfied smile spreading across his face.

Two minutes later, the man who had been sitting at the table returned from the restroom to an empty plate. He called the waiter over, demanding to know what had happened to his meal. The poor waiter hadn't a clue. But he did wonder why that nice young couple was hurrying out without even finishing their meal.

'TWAS THE NIGHT BEFORE NEW YEAR'S

—Nancy Kennedy

*I*t was New Year's Day. I put down my newspaper and stared across the breakfast table, marveling at my husband's composure as he ate his scrambled egg and toast.

Personally, I couldn't eat at all. I hummed. I whistled. I recited the Twenty-Third Psalm. But no matter how desperately I tried to block out the gruesome events of the night before, I couldn't shake the memory.

It began not unlike past New Year's Eves. My father-in-law was stretched out on the couch, calling out minute-by-minute time reports. ("Fifty-seven minutes 'til midnight! 11:04—just fifty-six more minutes!") Our two daughters were nestled, all snug in their beds, having overdosed on bean dip and Diet Dr. Pepper. Barry and I were curled up together on the love seat, struggling to stay awake ("just fifty-four more minutes"). When . . .

Crash! The noise came from our six year old's room. Barry and I ran upstairs to find it in total disarray with Laura jumping on her bed yelling, "Get him! Get him!"

Him was a mouse.

Barry lifted the edge of the bedspread to look under the bed. His eyes widened. I got down on my knees and peeked. We both shuddered.

A neglected banana peel, some empty candy wrappers, and a half-eaten sandwich offered an enticing salad bar for mice. I darted toward the door, only to be stopped in my tracks by a scary sound—the eek-eek-eek of a rodent. And maybe more than one. Outdoor temperatures had dropped suddenly, and Laura's bedroom had become a kind of Club Med for chilly mice from the big field next to our house.

"Shut the door!" Barry ordered, not wanting any furry creatures to escape while he moved Laura's bed away from the wall.

"You're gonna miss the ball drop!" hollered Barry's dad from the living room, where he was blissfully oblivious to the chaos upstairs.

Barry held his finger to his lips. "Shh. What's that?" He crept to the closet, mouthing, "He's in there." I bit my arm to keep from screaming while Barry eased open the closet door.

Wham! He smacked the floor with a rolled-up coloring book. Three mice fled into the room in three different directions. I grabbed Laura and pulled her with me up onto her bed. Barry stalked the room, the coloring book poised and ready.

Wham! Whack! No luck. The mice were just too fast.

"Hey, the ball's dropping!" came the report from downstairs. "Ten seconds!" my father-in-law called. "Nine. Eight.... Three. Two. One."

Wham! "I got one!" Barry yelled. At the stroke of midnight, as the entire eastern time zone celebrated the new year, Barry handed me the coloring book.

"There are more of them in the closet," he whispered. Then he opened the bedroom door.

"Don't leave me!" I begged.

"I'll be right back. I'm just going to the store."

It was just like one of those B-movies where the couple gets separated and one of them ends up with a limb gnawed off by a killer frog or a carnivorous cricket. I opened my mouth to protest but gulped instead, pointing out two mice calmly sitting in the corner staring at me.

I grabbed Barry's arm. "Let me go with you!"

"No, you gotta stay here." He pried my fingers loose. "I'll be right back."

The house grew quiet. Laura had escaped to the safety and quiet of our bed. Barry's dad snored softly on the couch. Alone in a room with rodents, I perched on Laura's bed, listening.

Rustle. Rustle. Rustle. Peering over the end of the bed, I saw two sets of tiny black eyes. With my heart pounding out of my chest, I clutched the coloring book and quietly raised it in the air. It was either kill or be killed, so—wham!—I missed them both.

Barry returned with a brown paper bag in his hand and a glint in his eyes.

"Look what I got," he said as he emptied the bag. "Two dozen mousetraps."

He set them everywhere—not just in Laura's room but all around the house. Snap! Snap! echoed from Laura's closet. Was the snap snapping Barry's sanity? He seemed a tad too enthusiastic for me. Suddenly, I was married to The Exterminator.

"I'm going to bed," I announced, not wanting any part of this testosterone-induced killing spree.

Barry grabbed my shoulder. "You can't go now. We're in this together. Besides, we're just getting started."

Just then a mouse ran across my toes—and the testosterone high took hold of me.

"Gimme one of those traps!" I cried. "Hasta la vista, Baby!"

SWEET SPIRIT

–Karen M. Feaver

*O*ne day while driving, my husband, Peter, and I got into a "marital adjustment session" (argument) on whether we could afford a new bedspread. This gave Peter the opening he'd been waiting for to share his views on fiscal austerity and its vital role in forestalling the imminent collapse of Western civilization.

I responded by recalling his recent purchase of a VCR–after giving the old one away because "the remote was busted." I pointed out that the remote control was miraculously healed once the batteries were replaced.

Some minutes into the battle of the bedspread vs. the VCR, my husband sensed the atmosphere had become decidedly chilly. So he thought he'd warm it up with a hearty chorus of "There's a Sweet, Sweet Spirit in This Place."

After belting out the first verse solo–during which I was completely unmoved–he looked over at me and exclaimed, "Now just the women on the second verse!"

SOMEONE TO WATCH OVER ME

–Janell Wheeler

*S*hortly after my daughter's wedding, I turned happily to the groom's mother and said, "It's such a relief to know Devri has someone to take care of her now."

With a startled look, she replied, "That's funny—I was just thinking how glad I am Phillip has someone to take care of him!"

ROMANTICALLY
IMPAIRED

—Nancy Kennedy

I used to think expressions of love came only in velvet jeweler's boxes, rosy bouquets, or boxes of Godiva chocolate. Now I'm married and I know better.

One anniversary, I hinted for weeks about a pair of silver hoop earrings I wanted. I left the catalogue open on Barry's desk with the earrings circled in red.

I even guided our conversations around to the subject with subtle comments like: "Speaking of the new tax laws, doesn't silver bring out the green in my eyes? And you know, the gold market's down, but . . ."

Finally, the big day arrived. No silver hoops. No chocolates. No flowers. But Barry did buy me new tires. "Nothing but the best for my girl," he beamed.

I could only wonder if his mother had dropped him on his head when he was a child.

"Do you like them?" he asked, still grinning. What could I say?

Barry spent the next hour washing and waxing my car. As he worked, I fumed and built my defense, in case I might be charged with murder.

"Your Honor, I killed my husband in self-defense. He's romantically impaired. He drove me to it!" I thought of past anniversary gifts: jumper cables, road flares, a snake-bite kit. The case for my defense was growing stronger.

But as I watched Barry scrub the dirt off my car, I remembered our first date, when he searched all over northern Maine for size-seven ice skates because he'd promised to take me skating. Then I thought about the time I hurt my back, and he cleaned me up and carried me in his arms to the doctor. He also lets me drink the last Diet Pepsi, and shivers in the cold after giving me his jacket to wear.

It's true he's never given me jewelry or roses, but Barry just speaks his own language when it comes to love. Flowers die, and chocolate turns to fat. Barry's gifts express his love by showing concern for my safety. And even if I haven't used the snake-bite kit and road flares yet, the jumper cables have come in handy.

Before my husband finished washing my car, I opted to let him live. I even grabbed a rag and helped polish the back bumper. It wasn't a Hallmark commercial, but it was romantic enough—even for me.

MIRACLE ON SECOND STREET

–Charlene Ann Baumbich

A miracle has taken place on Second Street, where George and I live. In fact, it is parked in our driveway. Perhaps the new car itself isn't the miracle, but rather the fact that George and I are still together.

You would think that by now we would have learned how to accommodate each other's polarized philosophies concerning major purchases. But instead, we have learned to gear up for the battle that will swallow us alive until the sales receipt is in our hands, thus disgorging us from the belly of the whale.

You see, George is a firm believer in easing into things, especially new cars. His shopping cycle goes something like this: read, explore, talk, compare, drive. Repeat. Notice the word *buy* is not in this cycle.

I, on the other hand, say, "Let's go buy a car—today."

And so, as the time to make a major purchase draws near, we begin by talking sweetly to each other, hoping that kind words and attitudes will ward off any similarities to past experiences. Which, of course, they do not.

Nevertheless, we cheerfully begin Phase One by independently browsing. George eyeballs a couple of makes on his way home from work; I venture behind-the-wheel a few times in showrooms during my daily outings. George picks up a couple of brochures; I form a few aesthetic opinions. We discuss our findings over dinner.

Already we don't agree. But in our unending quest to maintain peace, we cheerfully decide to give the other guy's favorite another look. Yuck.

This moves us directly to Phase Two: an exhausting search for possibilities. Evenings are spent prowling through lots, crawling in and out of cars that salesmen insist are just what we're looking for. Price tags continue to astound us. We play with the notion of keeping our old vehicle—until it coughs and sputters its death rattle, reminding us why we began this venture.

Finally, we enter Phase Three: I fall in love with a new model. It fits me like a glove. It has power everything. It has a moon roof, which is even better than a sun roof. It has a cool console with the gear do-jobby on the floor. It has leather seats and a four-speaker stereo system. Although I may be sitting perfectly still on the showroom floor, my mind is speeding us down the highway on a romantic weekend getaway.

Then I look at George and am slam-dunked into Phase Four: he doesn't fit in any car that fits me like a glove. He points to the top of his head, drawing my attention to the static electricity that has sucked his hair up to the bottom side of the moon roof. He thumps the side of his foot into the console to emphasize that consoles take up valuable space he needs for his size thirteen shoes. He thinks all radio programs are as good as audio bliss gets, so why do we need all those speakers? He says the engine is too small and babbles something about gear-ratio something or other. Our faces start to lose their patient grins.

Off to another dealer where Phase Five commences: George finds his dream car. It has loads of space and not a bit of extras. It has digital nothing. It's the worst color ever conceived by a human. Its ratios or whatever are all in order. It is the quintessential Old Geezer's car.

Which leads us to Phase Six: *What am I doing married to this person?* And our relentless pursuit continues.

Eventually, Phase Seven finds a place in our lives: a car we can both live with and perhaps even enjoy. It is a short-lived moment of bliss, however, because as we enter the salesperson's office, Phase Eight opens its jaws: the Sticker Price.

Thus begins the true test of our "for-better-or-worse" vows. We hold our breath, hoping the test-driver is actually able to return in our trade-in. Finally the driver reappears in the cubicle and shakes his head as he hands the keys to our salesman. It's downhill from there.

He names a price. We laugh. He asks us what we had in mind. We tell him and he laughs. Runs are made to and from a hidden manager. George and I squabble about what we each believe is a fair price to pay. I want this over so the rest of our lives can resume; George isn't making a deal until every deliberate step is taken during this car-buying dance.

Many people actually end up buying a car at this point. We don't. After five hours, *five hours,* we leave to find a "better deal." Phase Nine gulps us down: hostility. With car dealers, with one another. Why do we have to play this game?

About this time I announce I just can't take it any more, and George remembers yet another dealer we haven't tried. He'll check it out tomorrow on his way home, he says.

They have what we're looking for. We meet with the salesman that very evening and repeat our let's-try-to-buy-a-car scenario. After much bantering, this guy's best-deal price turns out to be higher than the last one. We drive home in our rattletrap, which suddenly feels conspicuously like a digestive tract.

George remembers still another place we haven't been. We decide we will browse the lot the next day, which is Sunday, when they're not open.

Eureka! "Car No. 2299" it says in bold black letters on a sticker in the window. I spring a new plan on George.

"How about this? Let's decide what we're willing to pay. You go to work tomorrow and I'll come here first thing in the morning with the checkbook. I'll hand them the keys to our car for a test drive while I tell them which car we want to buy. I'll offer to write the check if the price is right. I promise, George, I won't pay a penny more than we agree. What do you say?"

"Promise? You won't pay a penny more?"

"Promise."

"Deal."

At the crack of 9:00 A.M., I hand the salesman my keys and explain my plan. As he gives my keys to the test driver, he takes down some pertinent information. My heart thumps. The salesman gives me a price that's worse than the last one. I explain I'm disappointed. He asks me what price I had in mind. I tell him. He says, "If I can get you that price, you'll write the check?"

"Yes," I tell him.

He disappears and returns with the head honcho, whose fingers begin to tap dance on the calculator. He writes down a few things, then quotes me a price that is $91.28 higher than George's and my price.

"This is the best I can do," he says. "I can't even get rid of that twenty-eight cents."

I feel like I'm in a meat grinder. "Is my marriage worth $91.28?" I silently ask myself.

I ask God to give me strength. I remember saying, "Promise," to George.

What if I left and we didn't buy this car? Could our marriage take one more day of this? Absolutely not! How long could George stay mad? I grab a piece of scrap paper lying on the desk and act like I'm tallying up numbers to give myself time to think. Finally, but not easily, my conscience wins.

I put the checkbook in my purse and say, "I'm sorry you can't do anything about the twenty-eight cents, but it's the ninety-one dollars that has put me past what I'm authorized to pay."

I start to leave. The salesman shakes my hand.

"Deal," he says. "Write the check."

Some may say my shrewd buying tactics saved our marriage. I say the whale belched in the nick of time.

WHAT
A GUY!

–Marilyn Meberg

*E*ight years ago today, as I write, Ken Meberg burst through the portals of heaven, looking, I'm sure, for something that needed to be organized. He was a wonderfully competent guy who kept me aware of time and place.

I knew what time it was and where I was; I just didn't think about it much. To this day, I live in the moment and frequently find it amazing one ought to be aware of things that aren't in the moment. Understandably, that characteristic was an occasional burden to my long-suffering husband, but his patience and creativity ultimately set me on a more balanced track.

When we were first married, my car would occasionally run out of gas. I knew intellectually that a car runs on fuel that must be replenished from time to time. But on the other hand, once the car had been gassed up, I was surprised it wouldn't stay full. The same inefficient law of nature extended to groceries. How on earth could we be out of Tabasco sauce; I bought some once.

One of the greatest challenges I contributed to Ken's life was during the third year of our marriage. We decided to obtain a credit card to help us in time of need (which happened to be at the end of each month). I found the card a wonderfully handy benefactor and began to avail myself of its generosity. My usual illogic applied to this card. I didn't seem to remember that what was purchased yesterday needed to be paid for today. Mercy, other things are going on right now.

Ken had mentioned the overuse of the card to me several times, and I had listened conscientiously at the moment. But, of course, that moment soon became past tense and . . . well . . . you know.

The doorbell rang one morning, and I opened the door to a stern-looking gentleman who asked if my name was Marilyn Meberg. After I owned up to that fact, he asked if he could please see my Talk of America card. That struck me as an odd request, but I innocently pulled it from my wallet, which was in proximity to the door. He asked if he could examine it. I mindlessly handed it to him. (Do not try this in your own home; only the professionally mindless are qualified to accomplish this feat.)

With a dramatic flourish, he pulled from his pocket a small pair of scissors and sliced the card in two. I stared at him in disbelief as he handed the two card pieces back to me. Turning on his heel he said, "That's what happens to card abusers!"

I stood rooted to the spot long after he disappeared down my walkway. Slowly, the scenario began to make sense. I started to grin, giggle, and finally guffaw. "Ken Meberg, you're good."

That evening I joined Ken in the living room to read the paper. "Hey, Babe," I said to the newspaper that shielded his face from me. "I had a fun experience today."

"Really," he said tonelessly without lowering the paper.

"Yeah, a guy came to the front door and, based solely on my good credit, offered me a MasterCard with a $10,000 line of credit!"

Silence.

"Well, what do you think?"

Lowering his paper, Ken said with mischievous eyes, "That didn't happen."

"Well, how do you know?"

"'Cause that's not what I paid the guy to do!"

"You character! You really hired some guy with a suit and scissors to come to the front door and discipline me?"

"Yup," he said, picking up the paper.

"Where on earth did you find him?"

"I'm not telling; I might need him again!"

I miss Ken. I've wondered if he's keeping track of me from heaven and knows that I pay the bills, manage my finances, never run out of Tabasco sauce (which is easy because I don't use it), and keep gas in the car. Not only that, I have one credit card that I pay off at the end of each month. I think he would be proud of me. He contributed enormously to "growing me up," and I'm grateful.

In addition to preventing my life from having its edges tinged with chaos, Ken made me laugh. I never knew for sure what he was going to do or say, but at least once a day he would whiplash me with giggle inspirations. Like the time he gave me a birthday present in a huge box that progressed down to a tiny box. In the tiny box was a little gold charm for my bracelet. Guess what it was? A small pair of scissors. What a guy!

I wish the verse in Isaiah 62:5 read, "As a bride rejoices over her bridegroom," rather than the other way around because that's how I still feel about Ken. Our rejoicing over one another was a sweet gift. But God's rejoicing over us is even sweeter. We come into this relationship with all the flaws of a young bride but also with all the wonder, trust, and love. God, in turn, helps us to "grow up" in him. What a God!

IN SILLINESS
AND IN HEALTH

–Liz Curtis Higgs

*M*arriage is more manageable with humor. Laughing relationships last longer, and couples who cut up create ties that bind for a lifetime. Sandy from Pennsylvania sees it this way: "After all these years of marriage, there's a sense of 'this-oughta-be-good!' in our approach to each other's idiosyncrasies. Laughter is just another way of saying, 'I love you.'"

Cathy was sitting on the couch when she heard the drier go off. She knew the clothes couldn't be dry yet, so since her husband, John, was in the kitchen, she called out to him, "Honey, please turn on the dryer, would you?"

Soon, from the other room, she overheard him saying: "Ooh, Baby, I love you so much. You're so beautiful. I love your lint trap."

"What on earth are you doing?" Cathy called out.

"Turning on the drier."

STOP THE TREADMILL, I GOTTA GET OFF

–Charlene Ann Baumbich

These days it's mind-boggling to begin an exercise program. Electronic bicycles, step aerobics, videos–the options are already staggering, and they keep growing by the advertising minute. But healthy is in, and a while ago my husband, George, and I decided to activate the garden slug that lurks in each of us.

We eliminated a few options immediately. Like expensive health clubs, for example. Forget the annual fees–those perky, multilayered spandex outfits cost big bucks, not to mention the fancy gym bags and high-powered athletic shoes. For George and me, it was a simple matter of facing reality: we're not trendy. We're also not rich.

So we opted for one of the least trendy–and cheapest–exercise options: walking every evening with Butch, the Wonder Dog. But a lack of sidewalks and decent weather, coupled with a lack of cooperation from our disobedient mutt, squelched this budding idea.

Did that stop us? Never! Our gymnastic minds were flexing for new options when my grandmother died and left me a small sum of money. "I know, George!" I announced. "I'll get us one of those rowing machines." So I did. I got on it once and rowed, and my sciatica screamed at me to "GET OFF!" I immediately bequeathed the machine to George, who ceremoniously posted the printed rowing machine routine on the wall at eye level. He also faithfully talked about his exercise plan. But Grandma's been gone four years now, and that's about how long the rowing machine has had a broken roller.

But broken roller or no broken roller, we decided we were going to start exercising if it killed us. All we needed was to find the approach that was just right for us. With a spirit of relentless pursuit, we went shopping for an exercise video. Believe me, many of them captured George's eye—mainly because of the "artwork" on the boxes. Personally, I can't understand why anyone would actually want "buns of steel." Imagine plopping down in your desk chair and hearing a sound reminiscent of "The Gong Show." I think I'll pass.

We left the steel buns on the shelf and purchased Richard Simmons exercise videos instead. I've sweated to the oldies now and again. But Big George says he's just not ready to clap his hands and jive; he still insists he's going to fix the rowing machine.

Meanwhile, my stress level (induced by guilt about all the exercise we're not getting) was calibrating at the high end of the scale. It was clearly time to stop dinking around and just do it. So George and I purchased a new treadmill. We brought it home and George said, "You figure it out and show me how to use it."

So I got started, and here's what I learned:

1. Rest up before you wade through the instructions. "Straddle belt. Attach heart monitor to ear. Determine miles per hour and other settings. Attach safety shut-off to clothing." By the time I'd finished reading the directions, I was already exhausted.

2. Never—let me repeat—*never* use electronic exercise equipment when you're home alone. I admit that I should have paid closer attention to the warning about hooking up the safety shut-off. Suffice it to say, I hurled myself off that belt more than once. When I told George about my run-ins with the basement wall, he made plans to install a floor-level phone so I could dial 911 from the splat position. However, I climbed right back on that bronco and have now tamed it. But I still don't ride it as often as I should.

Today, after a long series of fits and starts, George and I have moved solidly into the "we're not kidding" stage of planning to exercise together. Just the other day we burned off a number of calories by flapping our jaws as we talked about blissful trips of togetherness in our basement: me treadmilling every step of the way, and George rowing along right there beside me. Or, since we also have one of those round things that looks like a miniature trampoline, maybe we could just hop a few miles together.

We're expecting big things to happen, and just between you and me, we might even make our own video. It'll feature George and me, lean and lovely, smiling on the cover. We'll call it "Mr. and Mrs. Buns of Steel."

Or maybe we'll just call it "The Gong Show."

THE BATHROOM
THAT ATE
OUR BUDGET

—Nancy Kennedy

*W*e only intended to paint the bathroom. Nothing fancy—just plain old latex, semigloss, easy-clean white.

That was before we had an idea.

Barry and I have kicked around lots of ideas over the past seventeen years, and most of them have been pretty good ones, especially those for "when we get our own home."

You know how it goes. You're sitting on the couch together, and one of you starts off with, "When we own our own home, let's have a fourteen-by-twenty-two-foot bathroom with double toilets and sinks and a sunken whirlpool tub that seats twelve and a big bay window that looks out on a pine forest and snowcapped mountains."

Then the other one says, "Yeah, and we can have piped-in music and a dimmer switch for the crystal chandelier and a little refrigerator stocked with freshly squeezed orange juice and a microwave to heat up those baby quiches."

Then, one day, we bought a house and had the chance to turn our ideas into reality. Sort of.

Our fourteen-by-twenty-two bathroom measures ten-by-five. Barely big enough to squeeze in *one* toilet, *one* sink, and *no* tub, only a shower. A shower with a shower head that was aimed straight at the top of the glass door, which meant most of the water shot out over the top (and onto the floor). Minor things we failed to notice when we bought the house.

No bay window looking out on a pine forest and snowcapped mountains either. It was more like a twenty-two-inch square with a view of an old bent oak tree and our neighbor George's horse-shoe pit.

So we readjusted our ideas.

"This bathroom wouldn't be too bad with a fresh coat of paint and maybe a floral valance at the window." That was our original idea.

As we prepped the bathroom for painting, I glanced over at Barry and noticed that look in his eye. I'd seen it before. It was his "I know we don't know the first thing about what we're doing, but I'm hoping that God takes pity on innocents and fools" look. He had it the time he entered us in a dance contest—when I was eight-and-three-quarters-months pregnant—and also the time he volunteered to chauffeur a group of squirt-gun-toting eighth-grade boys to Disney World.

This time, trouble entered our bathroom disguised as a question.

"Do you like this medicine chest?" Barry asked.

"Not really," I answered.

Next thing I knew, the medicine chest went sailing out the window, landing near George's horseshoe pit. It left a jagged, medicine-chest-shaped hole in the bathroom wall which, Barry assured me, would be almost as good as new with a little spackling compound.

Then he stepped back to study the room. "What do you think of the light fixture?"

"It's okay, I guess. . . ."

Boom. Down came the light.

"How about the toilet?"

Swoosh. Out the front door and onto the lawn went the porcelain throne.

"Now it'll be easier to paint in here," Barry reasoned.

He had a valid point, but I had the nagging feeling that something big was about to go wrong. Maybe it was the hole in the wall. Maybe it was the hole in the floor. Or *maybe* it was the way Barry eyed the vanity cabinet.

"I don't like that vanity, do you?"

The truth was I didn't, but I wasn't sure I wanted my husband to know that.

Even so, I did what I had to do. I picked up a crowbar and joined him in his demolition frenzy.

We took turns ripping apart the vanity cabinet. It was kind of fun—until we discovered that both it *and* the sink top were cemented to the wall.

This time it was my turn to contribute an idea. Shouting, "Let's replace everything!" I took a sledge hammer and smashed the sink top that jutted out from the wall. "What's more," Barry said, taking the hammer from me, "it'll be so much easier to paint in here."

With the third blow we found yet *another* little problem: no tile on the wall behind the sink or on the floor beneath it.

At the time, only *I* considered it a problem. Barry, the eternal optimist, saw it as an opportunity.

"You know, since we have to retile the wall anyway, I could knock out the top tiles in the shower and move the shower head over so the water won't go over the door anymore."

I looked at our shell of a bathroom and pondered the very real possibility that I'd have to bathe in the kitchen sink forever. So what if I had to keep mopping up after every shower? At least I'd *have* a shower. But before I could say anything, Barry had picked up an ax and a couple of power tools and started hacking away at the tile.

Hours later when the dust settled, I had a question. "Once you move the shower head, what happens if we can't match the tile?"

What happens is that tile contractors laugh at you. And then they hand you an estimate for $928 to remove and replace all the remaining tile in the shower, the bathroom floor, and the walls. To save $150, Barry decided we could remove the tile ourselves.

Finally, after weeks of hammering and chiseling, we tossed the last tile on the mountain of rubbish in the front yard. Barry stood back to admire his work and I stood back to sigh with relief. There was nothing left to destroy.

But our celebration of mass destruction was brief. It ended when I totaled the bills from our simple bathroom paint job. We had actually spent a hundred times more than we originally intended!

At the grand reopening of our bathroom, the tile gleamed and the toilet glowed. In fact, the entire room sparkled and shined. It wasn't the bathroom of our dreams, but at least I didn't have to put up with tile dust and hunks of wall in my hair anymore.

Then I saw Barry's face. There was that look again.

"You know, Honey," he said, "I was just thinking . . ."

Chapter Five
Just for Grins

Everything is funny as long as it happens to somebody else.

—Will Rogers

JUST CALL
ME LUCI

—Luci Swindoll

*O*ne morning I sat at the counter of a Big Boy restaurant not five minutes from my home. Newspaper in hand, I took the only seat left, next to a young man who was about halfway through his meal. We said nothing. After ordering, I opened the paper to scan the front page when I noticed out of the corner of my eye that he kept looking in my direction as if eager to talk, occasionally drumming his fingers on the counter. Finally, while still seated, he took money from his pocket to pay for his meal and, looking straight at me, blurted: "My wife just had a baby."

"Oh . . . how exciting. A boy or a girl?"

"A little girl."

"That's great. How can you just sit there so calmly? Why aren't you running up and down the street passing out cigars or something?"

"Well," he said, smilingly, "this isn't my first. She's our third girl. We have three girls now."

"And I guess you wanted a boy, huh?"

"Oh, well, yes. But, you know—I'm glad she's here and healthy, and that's what's important."

"That's right."

"The only problem is that we can't agree on a name for her. My wife wants to name her Lucy, but I don't know. I don't much like the name 'Lucy.'"

"Oh really? Why? I think it's a nice name."

"It sounds average . . . and, every Lucy I've ever known was big and fat. I guess I think when she grows up she'll be fat."

"Not necessarily."

"You know what I mean, you just have this preconceived notion. What do you think is a good name for a girl? What's your name?"

"Luci."

"Oh gosh, I'm sorry," he said, turning red and trying to smile. "Uh . . . can I buy you a cup of coffee?"

"How 'bout a hot fudge sundae?"

WAS THAT
A SNEEZE?

–Hope Mihalap

*N*ewspaper columnists are always on the lookout for fresh ideas. I often found new material by keeping my eyes and ears open to the simple physical facts of life, facts like burping and sneezing, for example. As I stopped by the newspaper office one afternoon to deliver articles, I heard the Sunday editor sneeze, "Ah-VRAKH!" I wouldn't have given the matter another thought had not the woman across the hall caught the bug at the same moment and sneezed literally, "Ah-choo, ah-choo, ah-CHOO!"

I hurried over to her. "Did you really honestly say, 'Ah-choo,' just now when you sneezed?" She remarked that she would scarcely consider sneezing any other way. The more I thought about it the more interesting it seemed. And it might not, I mused, be all that far-fetched because I myself say literally "HIC-cup!" when I hiccup. But most sneezes are not as easy to spell as hers.

My father's sneeze was legendary. He snorted, "Broo-CHOW!" If the grandchildren were around he would extend it to "Broo-chow-chow-CHOW!" in an effort to get a rise out of them. At first they used to jump up and down in delight, but as they became older and more blasé they would murmur vaguely, "Papou sneezed," and go on with their games.

Although my father's broo-CHOW had been known to fell a floor lamp, he disapproved of too loud a sneeze on the part of another. For years my mother stifled her sneezes into a strangled "Rukh," hoping he wouldn't hear. Then, as the women's rights movement came into its own, she read that it was not only assertive but healthier to let the old sneeze out with gusto. Accordingly she would bellow, "Ah-RAKH!" with the best of them causing my father to thrash apoplectically out from behind his newspaper to shout "Hah? What? What happened?"

I myself like an assertive sneeze. There is something abnormal to me about a gentle "pip" into a handkerchief. I enjoy embellishing my sneezes with an international flavor. Some days I choose Russian composers: "RachMANinoff!" I sneeze. "TchaiKOVsky!" Or "GLINka!"

As for geographical sneeze sounds, when I first learned that there was a Hawaiian island called OAHU, I realized that this was a sneeze just waiting to happen.

All of which reminds me of a woman I knew in college who burped, "OP'ra glasses!" I was fascinated. Some people may consider burps an indelicate topic, but I have heard that in some countries a generous burp at the dinner table is the highest compliment that can be paid the hostess.

In any case, some talented individuals can burp at will. I have never had this talent and, in fact, cannot even burp against my will. Only once was I betrayed in this respect and that was on an occasion in the Vassar College library.

There I sat in the decorous stained glass silence of the reserve book room, surrounded by dozens of stony meditative readers turning pages silently. All of a sudden I was aware of a ticklish sensation in my throat, and I remember thinking, *Now if I had ever been known to burp this would probably be a burp about to come forth.* But since I had never burped, I assumed it would be a yawn and opened my mouth accordingly.

"BURP!!" I roared at a volume unparalleled in grossness sending reserve books flying to the floor, shattering stained glass panes, causing fellow students to fall from their chairs.

I have never been able to do it again.

But you should hear me sneeze in church!

A HEARTY
HA, HA, HA!

–Barbara Johnson

They say three kinds of people populate the world: those who can count and those who can't. As you can see, I'm in the latter category. As I always say, give me ambiguity or give me something else.

Despite my math deficiency, uncertainty, and puzzlement, there's one problem I don't have. I'm not like certain pious Christians who suffer from the haunting fear that someone, somewhere, may be happy. I'm out to be a joy germ!

We have to be on the lookout for fun, whether it be in simple things like funny signs ("Our fish are so fresh you want to smack 'em!"); funny names (if Fanny Brice had married Vic Tanny, her name would have been Fanny Tanny); or funny bumper stickers ("Forget about World Peace–Visualize using your turn signal").

Just today I called my friend, Mary Lou, who at one time in her struggles was so far out you couldn't even find her with radar. But she has a marvelous sense of humor, and we have laughed and cried together many times. I've learned a lot from her about coping. But today she caught me off-guard. She told me that when she really feels down she has a special way of lifting her spirits. I waited for her to explain, expecting some spiritual gem to fall from her lips. Instead, she told me, "I get out an old Shirley Temple video and a box of chocolate chip cookies and lie down for a couple of hours to escape."

Maybe some time with Shirley will perk you up too. You might want to substitute Ry-Krisps for the cookies so you don't have to roll in the door when you reenter reality. Of course, some people say reality is a crutch for those who can't handle drugs.

But according to my calculations, reality is this very second. You see, yesterday is only a memory, and tomorrow is merely a dream. Today is an illusion. That leaves this one second. Every day you have 86,400 seconds. But they come only one at a time. In your bank account of time, no balance is carried over until the next day. You use those seconds or lose them. There is no chance to reinvest.

Make your investment wisely by believing you deserve to be full of joy this very second. And you can be. Decide to be. Don't put if off until you finish your chores; instead, make tedious tasks a game. Compete with yourself. Reward yourself. Make work play.

Be curious about everything and everyone. You'll get tickled in the process!

Trust the heavenly Father of Goodness. Giggle at his artistic genius in the world. Always remember you're created unique—just like everyone else!

I tell you, I'm not going to fret just because a neighbor is a few fries short of a Happy Meal or another driver on the California freeway doesn't have all his corn flakes in one box. So what if my chimney's clogged and my husband's belt doesn't go through all the loops? As a born-again believer, I have accepted God's forgiveness in the salvation of Jesus Christ, and I can freely forgive others and joyfully move on. Learning all I can from my mistakes, I better tolerate the mistakes of others. If there is a problem I can't change, with the Lord's help, I turn it into something beautiful.

Yes, joy is free, but it doesn't come cheaply. It's based on who I am, not what I have, where I'm headed, or where I've been. It's a biblical choice, and it's the best option—every single second of the day!

TELEMARKETERS AND OTHER SUPPERTIME ANNOYANCES

–Chonda Pierce

*A*fter we bought our home, I realized that all those papers we signed at closing were not legal documents at all. No, they must have been phone lists. Nearly every evening we get calls from telemarketers.

The scripts go something like this: "Hello. Allow me to introduce myself and the reason I'm calling." (Legally they have to say something like that.)

I know these are just people trying to make a living, but I'm trying to eat my pot roast, not comparison shop for insurance at the dinner table.

I have friends who hang up on them. Others who blow whistles in their ears. But I can't do that. I prefer a more subtle approach. I start by asking lots of questions before the telemarketer has a chance to finish his introductory speech. For instance, the other night someone called about installing a security system in my home.

"I just wanted you to know that for a limited time we are offering free installation," the young man said.

"Free?" I asked.

"That's right. We have service representatives in your area right now, and they would be glad to come out and explain the system to you."

"What system?"

94

"Why, the one we are selling and offering to install for free," he answered.

"How do you know I haven't had one installed already?" I asked, making my voice thick with suspicion.

"I . . . er . . . I don't," he said. "Do you?"

"Why would I tell you that?"

"Because I just want to know if you have one or not—to see if you would be interested in buying one from *us*."

"How do I know you aren't some cat burglar calling every house in the neighborhood to see who has an alarm system and who doesn't? And as soon as I go to sleep you're going to sneak in and steal everything I own. How do I know that?"

"Well . . ."

"You say representatives are in my neighborhood right now?"

"Yes."

"How many?"

"A couple, maybe."

"What are they driving?"

"I . . . ah . . . I'm not sure."

"If you seriously believe I'm so interested in security—and assuming you aren't a cat burglar—then why would you think I'd let a total stranger into my house? What sort of security business are you in anyway?"

"Well . . . these are home security systems that—"

"How did you get this number?"

"I . . . er. . .I'm not sure. It was here when I got here."

"When I say, 'The fat man walks alone,' does it mean anything to you?" I asked.

"Not really."

"Who's Abbie Hoffman?"

"I don't know."

"Where's Jimmy Hoffa?"

"I don't know."

"Was anyone on the grassy knoll?"

"What grassy knoll?"

"And you claim you're in the security business!"

"Look, ma'am, perhaps we're not the security service for you," he said. "As a matter of fact, I'm taking your name off the list right now."

"What kind of list do you have there, young man?"

"Just a list ... list," his voice cracked on the second list. "But I'm destroying it right now. As we speak. Hear that?" And I could hear the sound of paper being ripped. "All gone. I'm sorry I bothered you."

I softened my voice a little and said, "Hey, I appreciate that. And just between you and me, if anyone asks, this conversation never happened. Okay?"

"Okay."

Then, with a shot of panic I screamed out, "Oh my goodness!"

"What? What?"

"Someone in a dark blue van just drove by," I told him, whispering. "Are your men in a blue van?"

Click.

I know it sounds like a lot of work, but it sure beats letting your blood pressure boil so that you choke on your pot roast. Besides, it entertains the kids. (And, believe me, that's not easy to do.)

Has anyone ever called to sell you burial plots? My, but they're fun people to talk with.

"I know this isn't a very pleasant subject to address," the young man who called said, "but what is even worse is the idea of leaving this entire burden to fall upon your family."

"What do they look like?"

After a long pause he finally asked, "I'm sorry, what do *what* look like?"

"The plots. The burial plots."

"Ah ... well, I'm not sure. Like any other plot, I guess."

"Well, are they grassy?"

"Maybe. Probably."

"Then who mows them?"

"You know, I don't know. I can have a representative come by and explain everything. We have some in the neighborhood right now, and I'm sure he'll have pictures and samples and stuff."

"Do you sell plot covers?"

"Covers?"

"Yeah. I don't want my plot to get all muddy and nasty. I'd like to keep it covered and dry. You know, in case people should come to visit after church, and they're wearing their good shoes."

"I've never had anyone ask about covers before," he said. "But I can check on it for you."

"That's okay. Let me ask you this: If I buy a plot now, can I use it—I mean before I die. You know, to have picnics, family reunions, things like that?"

"I—I'm not sure. It's just a plot—in a cemetery. And I don't think it's very big."

"How far apart do the stakes have to be in a game of horseshoes?"

"I don't think the plots are *that* big."

"Then maybe I should buy several—end-to-end, though, and not side-by-side," I added.

"I think I can do that." But he didn't sound too sure.

"Do these plots come with a guarantee?"

"Guarantee?"

"Yeah. Like if I buy a beautiful, grassy, sunny spot and I die, how do I know you won't bury me somewhere else, like next to a toxic waste dump or something?"

"We don't bury people, ma'am. We just sell the plots."

"Do you sell a lot of plots?"

"I think we sell a lot of plots."

"How many plots in a lot?"

"I don't know. A lot."

"Maybe not."

"Uh . . . listen," he sounded more frustrated than ever. "I can send some representatives right over, and they can answer all your questions."

"About those representatives . . ."

"Yes?"

"When things get kind of slow around there . . ."

"Yes?"

"They don't like, you know, *hurry* things along, do they?"

"If you are implying that they—"

"Oh my goodness!" I shouted.

"What? What?"

"Someone in a dark blue van just drove by," I told him, whispering. "Are your men in a blue van?"

Click.

OFF IN
LA-LA LAND

–Barbara Johnson

*W*hen I was preparing to undergo some minor surgery recently, the doctor warned me the anesthesia might make me a little goofy even hours after the surgery was completed. For a moment I wondered whether anyone who knew me and thought I was already pretty goofy would even notice. Then I remembered that it's my husband, Bill, who's the peculiar one, being an only child and all.

The doctor said that when I left the hospital I was not to drive a car, sign any contracts, or make any irrevocable decisions because I would be considered legally drunk for twenty-four hours after the surgery. Never having had a drink of alcohol in my life, I had no idea what to expect. *Just think*, I told myself, *you're gonna be drunk without even taking a drink!*

The idea was so amazing to me that I started imagining I was drunk even before the surgery started. When I arrived at the out-patient desk, the receptionist shoved a stack of papers toward me and told me to "fill them out, check the things that apply, and then sign here, here, and here. Be sure to press hard, because it's a triplicate form."

In my imaginary state of drunkenness, I had a little trouble following her rapid-fire instructions, but I finally completed them all.

In just a moment the door opened, and a nurse called me in. As soon as she had me settled in a bed, three other nurses slipped through the curtain.

"Oh, Mrs. Johnson," one of them said in a low, excited voice, "we're so thrilled to have you here. When we saw your name on the admittance forms and realized it was you, we called you back early. All of us have read your books. I even have one of them here and I was hoping you would sign it for me."

I wanted to beg off, pleading imaginary drunkenness, but since she was a nurse she would know I hadn't had any anesthesia yet. So I signed her book and then looked at the four of them expectantly, wondering what would happen next.

They stood around my bed, their faces glowing with friendly smiles. Suddenly my little cubicle had taken on a party atmosphere. I wondered if it was because I was drunk—and then I remembered I wasn't, at least not yet.

"Barb, could we pray with you before your surgery?" one of the nurses said. Enthusiastically, the four of them joined hands, and the two nearest me clasped my hands in their own, and they prayed the sweetest prayer I'd ever heard. (Of course I thought I was inebriated, so just about everything was sounding pretty good to me then!)

Outside the curtain, I heard a man clear his throat. "Oh, Dr. Brown!" one of the nurses said, peeking out of the curtain. "We're just saying a little prayer for Barb. Would you mind waiting a minute?"

Evidently he agreed, because she returned and the prayer continued.

In just a moment the nurses' prayers ended, and the anesthesiologist stepped up to my bed and gave me a reassuring pat on the arm. He too said a little prayer, asking God to be with all of us in that operating room. Under ordinary circumstances I might have become a little apprehensive, knowing the moment had come for the surgery to commence. But he held my hand, and in my imaginary drunkenness—and having just heard the nurses pray for me so thoughtfully and sincerely—I managed to flash him a smile before the lights went out . . .

To be honest, I don't think I was ever "drunk" during those twenty-four hours after my surgery, but I certainly was on a high. I kept remembering those thoughtful nurses and how they had surrounded me with their love and held my hands in theirs—and then sent me off to La-La Land with their prayers echoing through my mind and filling my heart with peace. The joy that memory brought me erased any discomfort the minor surgery might have caused.

By that evening, I was feeling fine—and even a little mischievous. Knowing Bill had been warned by the doctor to beware of my expected intoxication, I could tell he was constantly watching me out of the corner of his eye. For just a moment, I was tempted to put a lampshade on my head and dance a jig on the sidewalk, then call up a real estate agent and sell the house. But just imagining how startled Bill would be was enough fun. And besides, being peculiar is his job.

PERFECT PITCH?

—Hope Mihalap

*M*y favorite story about noisy plumbing concerns a young opera singer at Tanglewood, the Boston Symphony's summer music camp. The director of the opera workshop told me how this talented soprano had to sing a role that included a long and difficult unaccompanied passage. A woodwind in the orchestra provided her the pitch, and she proceeded solo from there.

One night, the singer launched abruptly into the passage without waiting for her woodwind cue. Worse, she started singing four notes too high. The conductor waved his hands at her frantically to no avail. In a moment, she realized her mistake as the musical phrases became too high for her voice. She burst into tears and the curtains were closed.

The conductor ran backstage to find her sobbing in the wings. "What happened?" he cried. "Why didn't you wait for the pitch?"

"The oboe *gave* me the pitch," she cried, "and it was wrong! He gave me a high note that was wrong."

"But he didn't! You started singing before he even played."

At this juncture in the argument, someone back in the ladies' dressing room flushed a toilet. As the cheerful old commode filled, it gave forth a shrill, piercing, "Eeeeeeeeee."

"That's it!" cried the soprano. "That's the pitch I heard!"

That night, a musical commode had brought down the house!

I KNOW GOD
IS NOT A GRUMP
LIKE ME

—Cynthia Yates

If I were God, I would have a housekeeper. And paint my toenails red. Someone else would do the laundry and cook the meals. Quite frankly, I would expect to be waited on. And I would eat anything I wanted. Mostly Rocky Road ice cream and spaghetti. My cupboard would be crammed with gourmet potato chips and expensive chocolate. I would have a perfect size-ten body and hair that shone and swished like tall ripe wheat on a breezy day whenever I moved my head. I would never have to shave my legs, blow my nose, feed a fever, starve a cold. That's if I were God.

I would take naps every day. And vacations. I would spend a lot of my time traveling to the neat places I made: waterfalls and mountains and deep-forested woods. Yes, I'd have picnics in the woods, picnics without mosquitoes or ants, because if I made them in the first place, I could unmake them on the spot. Poof! I would simply eliminate anything annoying or troublesome. And I would keep the temperature to my liking: just warm enough to leave my sweater at home, sun that doesn't force a squint, the harvest moon would be my lamp every single night.

I'm sure I would be a good god. Not the kind of bad god you read about in mythology. I wouldn't turn anybody into a tree or a stump or something like that. Of course, I wouldn't have to worry about my creatures loving and adoring me because I would just zap them if they didn't. I would be queen. Queen god. I think that's what I would tell people to call me—Queen god, and, of course, they would obey. I would own everything. (Well, that would make sense, since I MADE it all anyway.) I would live in Queen god's house—really it would be like a whole planet—and there would be a huge solid steel fence, sky high, all around. No one could bother me, because, after all, I would be busy being Queen god and reading all the books I've been meaning to get to. I would command my angels to take messages and handle emergencies.

"Private" the sign on my stainless-steel gate would read. (I like to be alone—not always—but enough that I would post my hours.) "Queen god is available for counsel, for supplication, and to answer prayers at her convenience, usually between the hours of one and three each afternoon. Except weekends and holidays." In spite of my limited availability, I am sure I would be a generous and kind god.

Or would I? Well, at least I would be nice to the people who were nice to me. But if anyone disappointed me, I might just up and leave the planet. (Come to think of it, I can't think of anyone who has never disappointed me.) Anyway, Queen god would no longer be available to bother with anyone because her feelings would have been hurt.

In fact, Queen god might be a very grumpy god. And a grumpy god would be selfish, unreachable, and vindictive. Perhaps I should rethink this whole divinity bit. Maybe I don't really want to be Queen god, even for a day.

Come to think of it, why should I, or anyone for that matter, ever want to replace the real God, the only One who is always powerful, loving, and good? "Do not I fill heaven and earth?" declares the Lord—the Mighty One, Creator God, Holy God, King God!

Thank heavens, I think to myself, *I guess I don't need to be Queen god after all. Now where did I put that pesky scepter? I better get rid of it right away, before I do something really silly—like maybe turn myself into a frog. Yikes!*

Chapter Six

I Am Mommy, Hear Me Roar!

My mother had a great deal of trouble with me, but I think she enjoyed it.

—Mark Twain

TEETERING ON THE VERGE OF WILD WOMANDOM

—Becky Freeman

I am, at this moment, living every mother's fantasy. I'm all alone (going on the third day) in a rustic cabin, in the fall of the year. For three days, I've experimented with what life might be like if I were a single woman—and a hermit. Since I married at the tender age of seventeen and went straight from being someone's daughter to someone's wife, the ways of living alone are as foreign to me as the habits of some ancient tribe in a far-off land. I'd been wondering, especially after a succession of intense, crowded days (like the two I'd just spent in Hollywood), *What would it feel like to live in solitary isolation awhile?*

Now I know.

It's a little queer, even a bit lonely, but on the whole—for a short time, at least—it's rather heavenly.

I find it fascinating to be preparing meals for me and only me. I've also pondered, *What would I eat for meals if I were single? What would I buy at the grocery store with only my tastes in mind, left alone to eat whatever my heart (or tummy) desired?*

105

So far, I've gone through half a bag of apples, half a pint of caramel dipping sauce (fat free), a bag of chocolate cookies (fat free), half a can of turkey chili, half a can of baked beans, half a can of bean dip and assorted (fat free) chips, and two small potatoes. Oh, I did have a salad and some carrots (fat free) once – thrown in for good measure. My dinnerware has consisted of one sturdy Styrofoam plate, a small, empty butter tub, and a coffee mug. (These too, may I point out, are fat free.) The sole utensils in this cabin are a huge serving spoon, a fork, and a steak knife. I have eaten oodles of onions on everything with nary a thought of offending anyone with bad breath. Being a recluse has its perks.

Another thing: there is no reason to put on makeup or even shave my legs. Whom am I going to impress? Whom will I rub up against? I only comb my hair to get it out of my eyes, and I secure it back with whatever is handy – I've discovered a large Chip Clip or a couple of wooden clothespins work great.

I've undergone a rare transformation in these few short days. I'm becoming more than Becky of the Boonies; I'm turning into Wild Nature Woman. I've left the society of Women Who Run with Poodles and joined the pack of Women Who Run with Wolves. All day long yesterday I wore a shirt with a big ketchup stain right in the middle of my stomach. Slept in it last night. Who cares about stains when it's just you and the foliage?

Yesterday the most exciting thing that happened was that a huge praying mantis and her mate crawled atop my computer. I put them in a glass container, with the lid slightly ajar, for scientific observation. I heard somewhere that once the female is finished mating with the male she eats his head off. I guess I'll never know. When I woke up the next morning, both of them were gone. I guess they ate each other.

Actually, the subject of male/female difficulties brings me to how I landed in these woods – like some displaced Goldilocks – in the first place. I'm telling everyone that I'm away to write and reflect and catch up on work. (Though, so far, there's been more "ketchup on my work" than "catch up on my work.") If the truth be known, I'm actually in exile. Two days before I landed in the wilderness, I had a semi-nervous breakdown. It worried me because I didn't think it had a thing to do with hormones. Didn't feel like hormones. Just felt as though the world was falling apart, deadlines were looming over me like monsters, and my head was about to explode.

Scott discovered me curled up in the fetal position, crying and sobbing like a baby, saying over and over again, "I just can't do it all!" Another peculiar symptom: suddenly, I was seized with an overwhelming desire to have my house clean—*spotlessly* clean. *Immediately!* (Me, whose first book described me as the happy, oblivious owner of the "dirtiest floor in America." Suddenly, one little sock on the floor grated on every nerve in my body. The dust on the coffee table looked as thick and deep as the Sahara desert. It was all so hopeless, hopeless, *hopeless!!!* But I did not think it was PMS.

Scott found me in this pitiful condition and held me with compassion as if I were a child in his arms. He immediately set to plotting how he might creatively put me in solitary confinement for a few days. To his everlasting credit (young husbands take note), he did not mention the words *hormones* or *PMS*. Wisely, he said, "Honey, what is wrong with you is that you are worn out. You need time away to regroup, catch up on sleep and your writing. There's a cabin I know of that you can use for a few days. I'll take care of the kids, and you go and relax...."

"But, Scott," I blubbered, wiping my tears. "I can't possibly leave you and the children...."

"Oh, but I insist, Sweetheart. Really. You need this."

"You are the most giving man I've ever met. I love you so much."

"There, there," he patted my back soothingly. "Can I help you pack your suitcase right now? Warm up the engine of the car?"

That's when I started to get a little suspicious. Scott had the wild look of a male praying mantis desperately trying to save his own head. Obviously this "Momma's Getaway" held significance for the kids too. Maybe they knew instinctively that their mother was on the verge of Wild Womandom, a sight they preferred not to behold at close distance. At this point, who was I to quibble over motives? I was ready to do anything to help relieve the pressure building inside. When I agreed to the isolation, my family gave me a standing ovation.

That very afternoon, I found myself cruising through the countryside amid the brilliant fall trees painted with yellow, orange, burgundy, and chocolate brown leaves. When I arrived at the cedar cabin, I unpacked a few things. Then with some surprise I realized—well, what do you know?—I'd miscalculated my cycle. It *had* been a touch of hormones after all! Then it dawned on me, if this had been Old Testament times, under Levitical law I'd have been routinely exiled like this—"set apart seven days for customary impurity."

I used to think, *How awful to be "put away" like you're something disgraceful just because it was your God-ordained female time of the month!* Now, I'm beginning to see the brilliance of such a plan. Oh, I might have protested the injustice of it all on some level if I'd lived back then, but eventually I believe it would have dawned on me that this shunning deal was not a bad arrangement for all concerned. True, the men probably felt slightly superior. But as long as the woman had a week off to go somewhere to sit and relax without having to skin goats or shear sheep or make stew, who cared? Could this have been God's gift to women—a seven-day monthly jubilee?

I keep envisioning that famous children's story where Br'er Rabbit (who'd grown up in the stickers and thickets) pleads with Br'er Bear, "Please, oh, please—just don't throw me in the brier patch!" Only I picture an Israelite woman hiding her smile as she says, "Please, oh, please—you're not telling me I'm unclean are you? What? You want me to just sit? Sit and relax, you say? I can't even lift a tiny finger to cook or clean or scrub pots or milk goats? How *terrible*."

Research indicates that the monthly cycles of women living together in a group (like college dorms or tribes) tend to synchronize until everyone is on the same schedule. Are you thinking what I'm thinking this might have meant for the women of Israel? *Yes!* Most of the women would be ushered off, quite possibly *together*.

Think about it. Jewish women could do Girl's Night Out, Slumber Party, Women's Retreat, Gobble and Gab—all without a trace of guilt. After all, they were being put away for their "uncleanness." What could they do but stoically make the best of their dire predicament? (Of course, the Israelite men and kids were probably living it up too—belching loudly, leaving manna crumbs and quail bones all over the tent floor.) Whatever the case, after having some time to myself to gather my thoughts, I've come to believe this "setting apart" business may be an old tradition that needs revisiting, whether it takes the form of a women's retreat or a day alone.

In the book *Wouldn't Take Nothing for My Journey Now*, poet and author Maya Angelou discusses the refreshment that comes from taking some downtime for ourselves. She writes, "Every person needs to take one day away.... Family, employers, and friends can exist one day without any one of us." Obviously, this was true for my family. They practically threw a parade to celebrate my departure.

Angelou continues, "Each person deserves a day away in which no problems are confronted, no solutions searched for. Each of us needs to withdraw from the cares which will not withdraw from us. We need hours of aimless wandering or spates of time sitting on park benches, observing the mysterious world of ants." (I wonder if mating praying mantises count?)

"If we step away for a time," Maya Angelou contends, "we are not, as many may think and some will accuse, being irresponsible, but rather we are preparing ourselves to more ably perform our duties and discharge our obligations."

Precisely! Does not a battery need to recharge? Does not land need time to lie fallow so that it might better nourish its crops? Do not caterpillars need their cocooning time to morph into butterflies? And doesn't a woman need an occasional jubilee-getaway to refresh her body and soul? I also believe every busy mother occasionally needs some time away in order to experience being hungry for the company of family again. Empty arms, now and again, help us appreciate how sweet two arms can feel when they are once again full of children (or husband).

Well, my time here at the Wild Woman Cabin is coming fast to a close. I must shower (and shave), take the Chip Clip out of my hair so I can wash, roll, and brush it clean. It's time to throw out the onion, brush my teeth, and chew a mint; to forage for a shirt without a tomato-based stain. Time to pack up the car with my books and computer, to say goodbye to the friendly forest and woodland creatures. Though I've thoroughly enjoyed my exile, I am ready for my return home. My arms are beginning to feel strangely empty. I'm also craving communication with something that's not mineral, vegetable, furred, or antennaed.

"A day away acts as a spring tonic," concludes Maya Angelou. "It can dispel rancor, transform indecision, and renew the spirit."

On this I must agree. I take my leave from this abode with my spirit renewed, indecision transformed, and my raging rancor dispelled throughout the woods instead of all over my family. Goodbye, Wild Nature Woman. I think I'm ready to prance with the poodles again.

"SNAP OUT OF IT!"

—Sue Buchanan

*O*nce when I was preparing to speak for a mother-daughter banquet, I asked my daughters what tidbits of wisdom I'd taught them that I could pass on to others. Big mistake!

"Tell them to snap out of it," Dana said in the shrill tone of voice she saves for me and me alone. "That's what you told me all my life. I'm in a permanent state of snap-out-of-it-ness. It's imbedded in my brain. I can see it now on my tombstone; 'Here lies the body of Dana; she died trying to snap out of it.' Mother, puh-leeze! Get a life! I'm not made of foam rubber!"

Sorry I asked!

"Tell them to say the 'magic word.' And to mind their Ps and Qs," was Mindy's answer. "And tell them if they don't, you'll knock their teeth down their throats. That's what you told me."

Sorry again. But it's true.

I had invited a rather proper older friend to go to lunch at a fancy little tea room and thought it would be okay to take three-year-old Mindy along—she always behaved impeccably. At least in the past she had always behaved impeccably. For some reason that day, though, she was acting terrible and was driving me crazy. All the way there, she hung over the seat whining and fussing; and all the way there, I was feeling the disapproving glances of my guest.

I could see I needed to take some sort of action fast or lunch would be a disaster. When we got out of the car (we were fortunate to find a place to park right in front), I grabbed Mindy by the arm, pulled her close (well okay, *jerked* her close), and said—in her ear, and through tightened lips—"If you don't straighten up, I'm going to knock your teeth down your throat." (You must believe me! This is absolutely the only time in my life I ever said such a thing to either one of my daughters.)

Mindy looked up at me with horror written all over her innocent little face, but with all the drama of a Hollywood actress, and loudly emoted: "You're [sob] going to knock my [sob] teeth down my throat? Oh, Mama [sob] please ... puh-leeze don't knock my teeth down my throat. [sob] I'll be good. I promise, I'll be good."

About then I turned, not only to see the look of horror on my guest's face but to meet the stares of twenty or so elegantly dressed ladies as well—mouths open, forks suspended in midair—who were lunching in the outdoor courtyard of the restaurant. Is there a travel agent for guilt trips?

A mother can't win. I once visited Dana's high school wearing a suede suit; her friends (the boys) said, "Who's the foxy chick?" Dana was embarrassed out of her mind: "Why can't you dress like the other mothers?" When I wore jeans and an old tee-shirt, she said, "Moth-ER. Why are you dressed like that?" If I drove the big car, she said, "Don't drive that; they'll think we're rich." If I drove the small car, she said, "Do you want them to think we're poor?" You really can't win.

If only you knew how hard I tried with those girls! I washed, I ironed, and I cleaned till my fingers were bloody. I picked up underwear from the floor, I made cookies (I washed my hands in between), sewed clothes, drove hook-ups, went on field trips, and did without so they could have nice things.

Just thinking about it makes me want to cry. But as the tears well up, I pull myself together and repeat to myself the words a wise woman once spoke to her children ... "Snap out of it!"

BAD MOMMY

—Marti Attoun

$\mathcal{I}$ve finally figured out this discipline business. Time-out, positive reinforcement, grounding, no telephone privileges, no TV, early bedtime—they all work. The problem is that parents have been disciplining the wrong people—their kids instead of themselves.

Here's the scene: the five year old stuffs sunflower seeds up the cat's nose, and what does he get?

"Five minutes in time-out!" Mom shrieks as she falls on the cat and checks for a pulse. The five year old slinks away for five minutes of peace and quiet. He curls up with Thomas the Tank Engine and konks.

Mom, meanwhile, administers mouth-to-fang resuscitation to a stray. Who deserves five minutes in time-out?

Parenting experts recommend one minute of time-out per year of child. According to that formula, I deserve thirty-nine minutes of time-out. Next time my kids act up, I want the punishment. All thirty-nine minutes of it.

Here are some more punishments I deserve:

No telephone. I fantasize about a day without telephone interruptions. No one could offer to send free burial-plot information, free books to review, free aluminum-siding estimates or free family-portrait coupons. No kid could call and whine about forgetting his lunch money. "And I'm so starving I could eat a rat, Mom. Please, you've got to bring my money."

No TV. Every oddball in America has already been interviewed by Oprah or Donahue. As for the exercise shows, what's so great about thighs of steel, anyway? Seems like they'd be pretty heavy to drag around.

Early bedtime. I know some mothers who would stick sunflower seeds up their own noses if they could be guaranteed an early bedtime.

Grounding. Wow, I'd have to park the taxi-van in the garage and ignore requests for rides to the mall, birthday parties, guitar lessons, and the discount store to buy felt scraps for art class, then back again to get the embroidery thread to go with it.

Positive reinforcement. I can only imagine this comment, "Swell job you did with this beef noodle stuff, Mom. We sure do love your cuisine."

The more I think about discipline, the more I realize my kids absolutely don't need it. I do.

HOW TO OBTAIN A LOAN USING YOUR CHILDREN AS COLLATERAL

−Kathy Peel

*W*hen my banker learns I've written something on the topic of family finance, he will no doubt call the Library of Congress to have my work reclassified as fiction. This guy has the personality of a bug zapper. To tell you the truth, I'm a little miffed at him at the moment. I think it's pretty tacky that some bankers send their customers discount interest incentives for new loans. And others give nice gifts for maintaining a minimum balance. My banker sends sympathy cards to my children.

I mean, the nerve of him to think I would overdraw my account on purpose just to aggravate his ulcer. I told him not to take it personally—that it's usually due to a simple addition or subtraction error, an automatic draft I didn't record, or the thirteen missing checks I forgot to enter in the checkbook.

But it still puzzles me how a person like me—who keeps impeccable records—could regularly be overdrawn. As soon as I write a check, I immediately grab a tube of lipstick or crayon and write down the approximate amount of the check on the back of a gum wrapper. And even if I do forget to record the amount of a check once in a while, I don't worry about it because I keep a fifty-dollar buffer in the account to fool myself. This works well unless it's the check for the mortgage I forget to record.

Actually, I have my own method of accounting to balance our checkbook. I drop the last digit, add my weight! (not the one on my physician's chart, but the one on my driver's license), multiply by the number of children under our roof at that moment, and divide by my shoe size. That's close enough for me.

Actually, I have made some progress toward keeping our checkbook balanced. I hired an accountant. But that didn't make figuring out our family budget any easier. Quite frankly, I think budgets are downright unbiblical. You probably already know this, but God did not create the budget. Nowhere in the Bible will you find God putting one of his prophets on a budget. No, God is a loving and generous God. The budget is a human idea.

But as much as I hate it, we need some sort of system to figure out how much money we don't have every month. To tell you how much it costs to keep my family of five fed would only make you think I'm a few shrimp short of a cocktail. I hate those women's magazines with articles about how to feed a family of six on ninety-six dollars a month. You show me a woman who can do this, and I'll show you a woman whose entire family is anorexic. The way my kids eat, ninety-six dollars gets me down the first aisle and halfway through the dairy case.

Since the cost of living seems to increase in our family by the hour, we've had to be creative about making extra money. One way we've increased our family income is buying houses, fixing them up, then selling them at a profit. We've moved seven times in the last twenty-two years.

The first stress-producing part of remodeling houses is applying for a loan. Few will argue that bankers consider those of us who fall into the dubious category of "self-employed" on the same level with lepers.

During one particular house-hunting venture, we began our search for a home loan at a local bank. The loan officer looked like Ken who had a wife at home named Barbie. He had perfect posture—so as not to wrinkle the back of his shirt—his nails were perfectly manicured, and he had a head of hair any televangelist would die for. But the hair on his neck was evidently not sprayed down, because it stood straight up when we mentioned we were self-employed. We didn't stay long.

Finally we found a loan officer at a large bank who was willing to work with us. We breathed a sigh of relief when we started the loan application process.

It didn't take long to figure out the word *privacy* had absolutely no meaning to this man. He wanted to know everything from our blood type and underwear size to how many times we brush our teeth each day. He called us every day for the next three weeks to ask more questions. I had to account for every penny I'd spent for the past three years. Trust me, this was no small task for a woman who uses her canceled checks for confetti on New Year's Eve. Feeling a little put out, I suggested to Bill we just take off our clothes and stand in front of his desk. He knew every other detail of our lives—why not all?

In what was obviously a great act of faith on the banker's part, he loaned us the money for the house we wanted to remodel. But you must understand that families like ours, who don't have a lot of extra capital to invest, must live in their house and work on it at the same time. This can be interesting—to say the least. Think about it. Have you ever seen a picture of a woman shaving her legs with a paring knife over the kitchen sink because the bathroom's torn up? Or how many photographs show an irate lady trying to track down the electrician who skipped the country after installing her ceiling fan with two speeds—off and hurricane?

After remodeling our last house, we lived in it for eleven years. This posed a definite problem for a woman who lives with four men who refuse to throw away their old toothbrushes.

"If we're going to put our house on the market, we'll have to clear a path so lookers can walk through," I said with authority.

They did not respond. I knew I'd have to be ruthless.

"Okay, boys, let's start with your things," I said. "I think we can probably live without this headless GI Joe figure...."

"No way you're throwing him away. He's my favorite guy," James countered.

"Fine. How about this stringless guitar? It's just taking up space."

"Don't touch my guitar!" Joel pleaded. "In five years I'm going to start my own band."

"Mom," John begged. "When you run an ad for the house, just don't include our room. That way, when we move out and the new people move in, they'll think they got a bonus room with the deal."

I want to insert here that I try—with God's help—to be a woman who always tells the truth. I've taught my children that half-truths or not speaking up when asked a question to which they know the answer is the same as telling a lie. With every one of you as my witness, I confess that when my teenagers asked if I had seen their collection of 538 bottle caps, I said I gave them to a man who came to the door holding a gun and wearing pantyhose over his head. When James couldn't find his treasure box filled with three years' worth of expired toy coupons, a paper-clip necklace, fourteen empty fast-food containers, an empty jelly packet, and seven jelly-coated pennies, I told him I had no idea where it was. (Well, I didn't have any idea which garbage dump it ended up in.) And to this day, when Bill asks me if I've seen his very favorite faded, stained, shabby, ragged, bedraggled, dilapidated work shorts, I quickly change the subject.

Once I cleaned out enough clutter so we could honestly advertise that the house had closets, it went on the market. For a woman whose kitchen is listed on Club Medfly's most desirable list, keeping things public-ready is no party. We asked our real estate agent to put "Call before showing" in our ad, so at least we could hide the breakfast dishes in the clothes dryer before people walked through. We learned that most agents did call—from their car phones in front of our house. Good thing the house sold in three weeks because we couldn't live life in fast-forward much longer without becoming the first family to suffer simultaneous coronaries. I'm telling you, when the phone rang we moved at the speed of light. We put dirty clothes under potted plants, threw wet towels in the deep freeze, and hid newspapers in the piano. When we moved, I found my checkbook in the waffle iron.

After signing away our valuables, any possible inheritance, and our children at the title company, we started loading up our belongings. We resembled the road crew from Ringling Brothers Circus. It took three days, but we finally got everything moved and we saved a lot of money by doing it ourselves.

Exhausted, we sat down in a circle of odd pieces of furniture and dedicated our house to God. We prayed that he would make it a home filled with love, joy, and good memories. I personally prayed that if any family member ever mentioned the idea of stretching our budget by remodeling and moving again, God would keep me from wringing their neck. So far, he's answered that prayer.

GUNG HO!

—Marti Attoun

My eighty-nine-year-old grandmother calmly carried a platter to the table for Sunday dinner when a foot suddenly whizzed by her nose and nearly knocked the crust off the pork chops.

"HYYYAAA!" a voice thundered.

"Oh, sit down and eat. You're upsetting the gravy," Granny said.

My family finally has learned to live in harmony with martial arts. My nephew, now twenty-six and wearing belts of leather again, led the pack of family karate kids. He was ten and garbed in his friend's baggy white *gi* when he approached his dad about taking *goju-ryu.*

"I'd like to take *goju-ryu,* Dad. I need to learn the art of self-defense."

"You're going to need it, son, if you keep wearing your mother's pajamas," his father informed him.

A few months ago, our own eleven year old suddenly realized he didn't know a flying side kick from a cartwheel.

"I really need to take *tae-kwon-do,* Mom," he told me in all urgency one night. "It'll teach me self-discipline."

"Self-discipline?" I asked. "You mean *tae-kwon-do* is going to teach you to pick up your dirty clothes and do your homework without me begging and bribing?"

He didn't answer. He was busy aiming a toe at a string of dirt fluttering from the furnace vent.

The worst part of karate, though, is the young defender requires an opponent to practice his takedowns and blocks.

"Please attack me, Mom," my son begged the other night as he bounced up and down in the kitchen in his horse stance. "Come on like you're really going to hurt me. I want to show you how a little guy like me can throw a big mama like you with just his thumb."

"Honey, I'm too busy to attack you right now," I told him as I arm-locked a frozen chicken and tried to pry its legs off. "Go ask your dad to assault you."

"Oh, come on, Mom. Be a sport," he pleaded. Attack me just once, please!"

I finally sighed, whirled around, and grabbed his neck. The frozen chicken slipped from under my arm.

"OWWWW!" he yelped. If the chicken hadn't smashed his bare foot, I'm confident he could have flipped me over his back with just his thumb. That's what we're paying for, right?

By the time I retrieved the slick chicken from under the table, I had exercised muscles that hadn't stretched since high school gym class.

I crawled out and slowly stood, panting, with my arms drooping between my legs and buckling knees.

"Lousy cat stance, Martha," my husband said, walking in. "You'll never make it to black belt with a form like that."

PRIVATE PARTS

—Karen Scalf Linamen

I'll be the first to admit that my husband and children are treasures that enrich my life to no end. I wouldn't trade them for anything the world has to offer. Do I want gold? Brushing and braiding Kacie's flaxen hair provides plenty of that. Elegant music? Kaitlyn's laughter will suffice. Fine wine? I'll take the kisses of my man any day. The finer things of life are already in my home.

But contrary to popular belief, the best things in life are hardly free. All this rich living comes with a price. Part of the cost, quite frankly is ...

... what's that word again?

Oh yeah.

Privacy.

It's nice to be sought after. But sometimes you can have too much of a good thing. My pet peeve is hearing a knock on the bathroom door followed by the familiar words, "What are you doing in there?"

What do they think I'm doing?

Maybe kids have this weird fear that, while their bath time is reserved for boring functions of elimination, grownups aren't bound by the same rules. Maybe they think we hide out in the bathroom so we can do really cool things we don't let them do, like eating Gummi Bears before dinner and watching cartoons when our homework isn't done. That's why we lock the door. We don't want our children to know we're having all the fun.

I knew a woman who once dressed her seven-year-old daughter as a "Mommy" for Halloween. She put curlers in her daughter's hair, smeared jelly on her shirt, and tied an apron around her waist. But the *pièce de resistance* was the baby doll strapped to her leg.

We all know what that feels like, don't we?

I don't know about your experience with little ones, but my babies didn't believe in pacifiers and security blankets. After all, why should they cling to a threadbare piece of cloth when they could cling to me?

Kaitlyn's comfort item of choice was my earlobe. She hung on when she was bored, scared, or tired. She considered my earrings a very personal affront.

Kacie got a little more personal than that. She's three and still thinks my right armpit belongs to her. That and my mole. It's on my left shoulder blade. One day she skinned her knee on the driveway. After I patched her up, she was still crying. I offered hugs, popsicles, gum, and more. She wouldn't stop crying. Finally, through her tears, she said, "I want your mole." She wrapped her arms around my neck, slipped a hand under my shirt, found my mole, hiccuped once, and stopped crying.

I teach my kids the concept of personal space and the idea that there are parts of their body that are private. For my daughters, I've described these areas as the parts of the body that would be covered up by a two-piece bathing suit. What I don't tell them is that this definition will apply until they become mothers. Somehow, in the process of conceiving a baby, birthing a baby, and nursing a baby, everything's up for grabs. Between husbands, nurses, doctors, and our newborns, every "private part" we ever had seems to become public property.

I remember when I was giving birth to Kaitlyn. I had just passed my pain threshold and asked—no, begged—for some drugs. In no time at all, the Demerol took effect and ushered me into la-la land. I know I was in la-la land because I remember looking at my husband and saying thickly, "Honey, could you close the kitchen door? I think I feel a breeze."

Was I in the kitchen? Of course not. That was the Demerol talking. Did I feel a breeze? What do you think? The way the LDR door kept revolving with hospital staff, gusts in that room must have been approaching 20 mph–and me wearing nothing but a paper gown and metal stirrups. No doubt wind chill was a major factor. It's a miracle I didn't have to be treated for frostbite at some point after crowning and before my episiotomy. Breeze? That's an understatement: I was experiencing high winds in an area of my anatomy where the sun never shines.

Privacy. Hah!

By the time we're mothers, we don't have any private parts left. The skimpiest bathing suit wouldn't reveal anything we haven't already revealed to total strangers in lab coats.

And what about privacy when it comes to our personal belongings? We spend years trying to teach our children the nuances of sharing. We talk about greed versus generosity, selfishness versus selfless giving. We model and lecture and teach and inspire. And after we have expended all our words on the subject, what our children manage to conclude from our vast outpouring of wisdom and insights is that what's ours is theirs and what's theirs is theirs too.

I remember once, when Kaitlyn was about four, feeling tired after a long day filled with Barbies and Big Bird. I felt like I needed a break from my role as Social Director and Principle Plaything for our daughter. She was begging me to play hide-and-seek when I spoke up in frustration: "Kaitlyn, we've been playing for hours! What do you think I am, a toy?

Kaitlyn looked at me and without batting an eyelash said, "Yes."

Well. That explains a lot, doesn't it?

After all, toys are on call twenty-four hours a day: they have no personal space and get no respect. They don't have any possessions. Half the time they don't even get to wear clothes.

But maybe I should count my blessings. I might not get any more privacy than Barbie, but at least my elbows bend.

Yep, if you're busy raising a family, privacy may be hard to come by. And yet, there's no denying the rejuvenating power of solitude.

Being needed is a great thing. And if we're in the midst of raising families and we happen to be needed twenty-four hours a day ... well, it's still great.

But to keep it that way, we need to renew ourselves with a little privacy now and then. Spend time with Jesus. Read about him in the Bible. Read his very own words in the New Testament. Sing songs for him. Then just be quiet for a while. Our hours apart can leave us refreshed and energized. They can remind us who we are. And they can give us an opportunity to focus and plan.

On top of all that, they just might leave us with a deeper appreciation for our families.

Even if they do get us mixed up with Barbie now and then.

FLEX TIME

—Marti Attoun

*S*pring forward. Fall back. It really doesn't matter at our house. For the thirteen years since we became parents, we've been operating under MDT—Mom's Daylight Time.

This is the natural time zone into which mothers everywhere drift if they want to keep their households running. At 6:30 A.M., a mother starts chirping, "Rise and shine, kids. It's almost seven."

At 6:45, when the little snoozers have yet to ooze from bed, she starts hollering. "Okay, kids. It's almost seven-thirty. You're going to miss the bus."

By 7:00 (according to the bachelor neighbor's clock), she's downright frantic. "The bell's going to ring at eight—and *you're going to be tardy!*"

My own mother actually finagled our clocks so my sisters and I were always in the dark as to the exact hour. Our mantle clock usually bleated a mournful half-song on the half-hour, finishing it up on the hour. But some mornings, especially Sundays, that clock went berserk and sang every ten minutes. So did Mom.

"Girls, get up or we're going to be late for church. You know we have to pick up Mrs. Trent." We knew that Mrs. Trent was still in her nightie, but we rolled out of bed anyway. It was impossible to sleep when Mom gave the oven its Sunday morning rack adjustments so she could cook a roast during the sermon.

Within ninety-six hours of becoming a mother, I switched over to MDT. It has a built-in burro factor of about fifteen minutes, which is crucial for new parents who must pack the diaper bag before every outing. The burro factor includes time to assemble the thirty pounds of baby accessories and make return trips to retrieve forgotten pacifiers. If you plan to be on time ever again in your life, you'd better be living on MDT.

Once you shed the diaper bag, bottles, and infant seat, you still need MDT for its built-in shoe factor.

"But I'm absolutely positive I took them off right beside the bed," says the barefoot child. Ten minutes later, he remembers kicking off the muddy tennies outside the front door. Prying the shoes from the jaws of the neighbor's hound takes another ten minutes.

Wise mothers never abandon MDT. It's quite precise at bedtime, curfew time, and dating time.

"Be sure you're home by midnight," a mother warns her teenage daughter as she leaves with her date. The mantle clock gongs, and the girl glances over her shoulder. "But, Mom, it's already 11:30!" she shrieks.

My, how time flies when it needs to.

SUIT
YOURSELF

—Candace Walters

*I*t sounded like a good idea initially—my sixteen-year-old daughter, Amy, and I would go shopping for new bathing suits together. What a great way for us to build treasured memories, I thought happily. But that was before I discovered how insane my idea really was.

Amy and I went to a large department store where all swimwear had been marked down forty percent. I realized Amy and I would have to "bond" with hundreds of swimsuits between us—she was looking at size six, and I was into the double digits on the other side of the department.

"How 'bout this, Mom?" Amy yelled across the floor as she held up a piece of blue material on a hanger. I gasped. Without my glasses on, the hanger looked bigger than the swimsuit.

"I think that belongs in hair accessories, honey," I said sweetly, muttering to myself about the gall of some swimsuit manufacturers. Meanwhile, I was having my own problems trying to find a suit that covered cellulite, stretch marks, and the weight I was still trying to lose from having my third baby (who's now in junior high).

"How 'bout this, Amy?" I called back, holding up a beige one-piece suit with a short shirred skirt and an empire neckline.

"Why don't you just wear a trenchcoat?" she answered, making a gagging motion with her index finger in her mouth.

We made a few more selections and took them to adjacent fitting rooms. Through the thin wall, I could hear Amy exclaim, "Hey, Mom, these mirrors are awesome! Let's get some for our house." I made a gagging motion with my index finger in my mouth.

A few minutes later, Amy tapped on my door. I opened it a crack and peeked out. She was wearing a neon pink, two-piece suit. It was painfully obvious she was nearly twenty years younger and twenty (okay, thirty) pounds lighter. Her thighs didn't even rub against each other as she strolled up and down the hallway!

"Come on, let me see your suit," Amy prompted. I was still in the fitting room hiding behind the door. It wasn't the suit I was worried about. I slowly opened the door to reveal a sarong-style Hawaiian print. Amy gasped and her eyes opened wide. "Does Dad know you look like that in a bathing suit?"

"Of course he does," I insisted. "And when you've been married twenty-five years, you'll understand what true love means. Besides, I looked just like you when I was your age, and you're going to look just like me when you are my age. My mother and I had this same conversation when I was a teenager."

Amy started to giggle, then laugh, then howl as she went back to her dressing room. I banged on the wall to quiet her down, but she couldn't hear me. And I thought I had taught her to respect her elders.

I don't know who writes the advertising copy for swimwear, but I suspect it's thin men. Here are some claims actually printed on the tags attached to the swimsuits: "Shirred leg openings create a slender silhouette." "Maillot designed to stylishly blur tummy bulges." "This modified high-cut style creates a lithe look." Who are they trying to kid? These must be the same advertisers who tell us ovens actually self-clean, permanent press doesn't wrinkle, one size fits all, and the Lamaze method makes childbirth painless. Try telling a man in a hospital gown on his way to the surgical suite, "Now, this won't hurt if you just remember your breathing exercises."

Our afternoon of gathering treasured mother-daughter memories dragged on. Amy tried on suit after suit, gliding up and down the hallway like a Miss America contestant. Sometimes she even dared to go out into the department to choose another style—still wearing a swimsuit! I always thought they should provide long robes in case you wanted to leave the fitting room without redressing or if the store caught on fire. I spent all of my time with the same six suits I'd started with, trying with each to squeeze it on, suck it in, and push it up. *At least my dressing room is neat,* I consoled myself. *I'm sure Amy's is a disaster!*

After two hours of being humiliated by the swimwear industry, my own figure from three vantage points, and my only female offspring, I'd had enough. I bought the same basic black style I always buy. Amy chose a polka-dotted, chartreuse maillot. However, we are never going to be seen together at the same swimming pool. She won't allow it—and neither will I.

My only hope is that Amy will someday have to shop for a new bathing suit with her teenage daughter.

Chapter Seven

Every Kid Has a Funny Bone

Insanity is hereditary—you get it from your children.

—Sam Levenson

FROM THE
MOUTHS OF
BABES

My five year old ran into some difficulty while trying to put on his full-body pajamas. "Jesus," I overheard him say, "will you help me get these pajama legs on?" A few silent seconds later he repeated more loudly, "Jesus, I said will you help me get these pajama legs on?"

After another brief silence, he said, "That's it! I'm telling your father!"

—Jeanne Michaud

One Sunday I asked my six-year-old Sunday school students to write a short prayer. Arthur stared into space, fidgeted in his chair, and chewed the end of his pencil before finally writing: "Dear God, please help me be the person my dog thinks I am."

—Wilette Wehner

A friend of mine used to teach Sunday school, and her favorite hymn to sing in class was "Oh, the Consecrated Cross I Bear." One Sunday, a concerned mother questioned my friend about a song her child said she'd learned in class. Her daughter had been singing, "Oh, the Constipated, Cross-Eyed Bear."

—Kirsten Jackson

My great-granddaughter, Melissa, six, was excited about being at her first wedding. When the pastor, the groom, and the best man took their places, she couldn't take her eyes off of them.

At the organ's cue, I directed her attention to the back of the church. Glancing at the front again and then at the bride, Melissa whispered, "Grandma, does she get to take her pick?"

—Clara Null

My husband and I had done our best to prepare our three-year-old son, Andy, for the arrival of his new sibling. We anxiously watched his reaction that first afternoon at the hospital when he met his little sister.

To our delight, he showed some brotherly interest. Then he turned to me and announced, "Okay, Mommy, put that baby back in your tummy and let's go home."

—Susan VanAllsburg

My granddaughter, Dawn, age four, showed me where her mom had planted some flowers in the yard. She explained, "Mom had to put some bulbs in the ground, so the flowers could see where to grow."

—Gwen Scherling

The other night at the supper table my husband and I were talking about a personal matter. We began spelling some words so that our two-year-old son would not hear.

He had recently begun learning about the alphabet and apparently he did not appreciate being left out of the conversation. He turned to us and nonchalantly asked, "Have either of you seen my L-M-N-O-P?"

—Beth Strong

We were trying to memorize Matthew 11:28, in which Jesus bids us come to him, promising rest. It sounded as though all my four children were getting the gist of it, until my younger son recited: "Come unto me, all ye that labor and are heavy ladies."

—M. L. Ackley

I was watching my five-year-old granddaughter, Christy, play with her dolls. At one point, she staged a wedding, first playing the role of the bride's mother who assigned specific duties, then suddenly becoming the bride with her "teddy bear" groom.

She picked him up and said to the "minister" presiding over the wedding, "Now you can read us our rights." Without missing a beat, Christy became the minister who said, "You have the right to remain silent, anything you say may be held against you, you have the right to have an attorney present. You may kiss the bride."

—Sonja R. Ely

When my daughter was in fifth grade, she showed up in the kitchen one Tuesday morning dressed in her finest Sunday attire. "Where's my Bible?" she asked.

"On the shelf in your room," was my quick but baffled reply. "Why?"

She replied sweetly, "It's Career Day, and I'm going as a mistress."

Being a wise mother, I knew that if she truly was going to school as a "mistress," she most certainly needed that Bible. "Do you know what a mistress is?" I inquired.

"Of course I do!" she stormed. "It's a female minister!"

—As told by a mom named Diana to Liz Curtis Higgs

On our vacation in Florida, the kids spent most of the time in the pool. After a few days, they began to look for ways to irritate each other. When two-year-old Jacob started to get in the pool with his sisters, they told him, "No! There's a shark in here!"

Jacob pulled back from the water. Confused, he looked around and then tried to get in again, only to hear the same warning. This went on for a while, and finally, Jacob gave up.

As he walked past my chair, I heard him mutter, "Get 'em, Shark."

—Kim Biasotto

Kelsey, my niece's five-year-old daughter, listened attentively to her Sunday school teacher read the story of the Good Samaritan.

"... They stripped him of his clothes, beat him, and went away, leaving him half dead." The teacher then continued with the rest of the story.

When Kelsey got home, she needed to clear up one thing. "Mamma, which half of the man was dead—the top half or the bottom half?"

—Donna Garrett

My three-year-old daughter, Katie, loves music. Doesn't matter if it's John Tesh, Lawrence Welk, P.D.Q., or Johann Sebastian Bach. As long as something has notes in it, she's humming it. But though she's good at picking up the rhythm and the beat, she doesn't always get the lyrics quite right. The other day I heard her singing one of her favorite Sesame Street numbers. But instead of singing "La De Da De Da, La De Da De Da, La De Da De Da Daaaa," as the song went, I heard her cheerfully belting out her version of the lyrics: "Naughty Naughty Da, Naughty Naughty Da, Naughty Naughty Da Daaaa!" I've always known my child was a musical prodigy, but, until then, I hadn't realized her brilliance extended well beyond the musical realm. Quite obviously she'd been plumbing the depths of human psychology, no doubt a student of the great Freud himself!

—Ann Spangler

My wife, Kelly, overheard our five-year-old daughter, Jordan, talking in a corner.

"Who are you talking to?" she asked.

"Myself," Jordan replied. "Mommy, can God hear us when we whisper to ourselves?"

"Of course," my wife said. "God hears everything."

"Oh boy," Jordan sighed. "I'm in trouble."

—Michael Amedick

I thought my husband and I had been good parents. So, I was shocked when my daughter called to complain after spending her first weeks at the University of Georgia.

"You raised me wrong," Amber said.

"What are you talking about?"

"You sheltered me too much, Mom. I'm shocked by everything!"

–Valerie A. Norris

WORMS IN MY TEA

—Becky Freeman

Some mothers use TV as a babysitter. Not Becky Freeman. No sir. The first thing every morning, I run outside our lakeside home, look for any small creature that breathes and moves, pop it in an empty butter tub, poke holes in it (the butter tub, not the critter), and my three year old, Gabriel, is set for the day.

There have been days, however, when I probably should have fallen back on the TV. One such day began as I sat folding the morning's wash. I noticed with a sense of unease a strange bulge in the pocket of a pair of Gabe's jeans. Gingerly, I forced myself to explore the warm, dark interior of the pocket, reminded of the feeling I had had years before when the bigger neighborhood kids would blindfold us little kids and force us to stick our hands into a bowl of cooked spaghetti, all the while assuring us the bowl contained either brains or guts. I realized, as I explored the pocket under discussion, that I hadn't matured all that much.

My hand enclosed an object that could have been a piece of bark. Feeling false reassurance, I extracted the mysterious bulge.

Can anyone know how black and shriveled and—well, bark-like a frog can be unless they have seen one washed, rinsed, and fluff-dried?

This event set the tone for the morning. Later that same day I turned from loading the dishwasher in time to see Gabe holding a baby turtle by the tail with one hand, scissors poised in the other.

"Whoa, Gabe!" I managed. "What do you think you're doing?"

His reply had a "Why do you ask?" tone to it. "This turtle needs me to cut his ponytail."

That turtle owes me one.

Toward evening that same day, things quieted down entirely too long. (Have you ever wondered why six minutes of peace and quiet feed the soul of a toddler's mother while seven fill it with terror?) On the seventh minute, I dropped my chopping knife with a clatter and ran out to the back porch to check on Gabriel. All was strangely calm. In fact, he seemed to be meditating, his gaze fixed upon a Styrofoam ice chest waiting to be stored away. Our eyes met when I heard a thumping sound issuing from the closed ice chest.

"There's a cat in there," Gabe said matter-of-factly, jerking his thumb toward the chest. I was not unduly alarmed for the safety of the cat at this point, since I could see the lid of the chest rise and fall with the thumps, but I did move to liberate the animal. As I lifted the lid, I realized with shock that Gabe had managed to fill the chest with water before depositing Kitty. I grabbed the saturated feline by its neck and estimated her to be on about her ninth life. I turned horrified eyes on my son. Like George Washington, he did not lie.

"I put her in there," he confessed. But he had a reason. "She was really thirsty."

Time passes, wounds heal (both to cats and to moms), and life goes on. For several days after that, nothing particularly unnerving transpired. Then one evening at church I looked down from my hymnal to discover that Gabriel clutched yet another wilting frog in his warm little hands. For some unknown reason, Gabe chose this moment to ask in a loud whisper, "Something smells! Is it you?"

Needless to say, I, Gabe, and the frog all needed "Amazing Grace" to survive that service.

But Gabe, our baby, is growing and is now big enough to dig for fishin' worms. What I wish is that he was big enough to go fish-ing with them, because he so hates to see them go to waste. Believe me, there is no experience that quite compares with downing the last of a big glass of iced tea only to discover a grayish worm squirming among the cubes at the bottom. "Just look," Gabe cooed sweetly as he showed me a sand pail containing a number of worms he had not yet invited to tea. "See how they love each other! They're hugging!"

But Gabe is maturing. Just yesterday he confronted me, hands behind his back with the look of love and pride other children have when they bring their mommies a hand-picked flower. Beguiled, I extended my hand where he lovingly deposited a snail, complete with slime.

"It's for you," he beamed. "I love you, Mommy!" Then he kissed me straight on the lips.

Take it from a woman who knows. Snails and worms aren't so bad. Really.

PERFECT LITTLE LADIES?

−Ann Spangler

*S*everal years ago I had the pleasure of knowing two precocious three year olds. Christine and Mo Mo were tiny, golden-haired beauties, cousins who were always chortling over some shared mischief.

One day Christine's mother hosted a lovely bridal shower. Both girls were decked out in fancy dresses and shiny shoes. Instead of chasing each other through the house as usual, they behaved like perfect little ladies.

Sweet smiles graced their chubby cheeks as they handed glasses of cool, clear water to the assembled guests. How darling they looked! How helpful they were! The women couldn't get enough of those cute-as-a-button cousins.

It wasn't until the plates had been cleared and the last guest had left that the story came out. Suspecting their ladylike behavior, one of their older sisters decided to do a little detective work. Following them, she discovered the awful truth. The two little girls had been grabbing glasses from the table as fast as they could, trotting into the bathroom and then dipping them with great gusto into the toilet bowl!

More than fifty women that day washed their cheesecake down with a libation of toilet water.

I laughed myself silly when I heard the story until an awful thought occurred to me. Had I been there that fateful day? That year was so full of weddings and babies I couldn't keep all the parties straight.

Even though the crime had been committed months earlier, my mouth tasted suddenly sour. The more I thought about it, though, the more certain I was I'd been spared that particular event. Suddenly, the whole story got me chuckling again.

Humor, like most things, is determined by one's perspective on life. But that day, whether you thought your glass was half empty or half full didn't matter a whit. In either case, you'd been had by a couple of perfect little ladies!

HOW WILL I
FIND YOU WHEN
I GET TO HEAVEN?

−Ellie Lofaro

*R*ainy days and Mondays don't always get me down but they sure make me sleepy. Especially when the rainy day is a gloomy, chilly Monday afternoon in late fall. So, at 3:45, I plopped on the couch with a magazine. I knew the house would come alive with dramatic stories, snacks, homework, permission slips, and the like at 4:02, as it does every weekday. *Lord, let these seventeen minutes stretch in a supernatural way. As a matter of fact, please stop the time, Lord. You've done it before. I really need a good nap.*

Raindrops were rolling down the den windows. Wind was blowing. Branches were swaying. Leaves were falling. The house let out an occasional creak. I read two lines and fell fast asleep. I was down for the count. As you may have guessed, the Lord did not answer my prayer. In what seemed like a minute later, the front door flew open with an announcement from my gregarious nine-year-old son, Jordan. "Maaaaaaa! We're ho-o-ome!" My daughter, Paris, a sophisticated sixth grader, just waltzed through and whispered, "Hello, Mother," without making eye contact. Close behind, as is her lot in life, came my baby.

Along with adding boatloads of joy and laughter to our home, six-year-old Capri makes me even more tired than rainy days and Mondays. She knows what she wants and when she wants it and never lets the big kids pull anything over on her. Capri is the one with a heavy Brooklyn accent even though we left New York when she was two. And with that accent, she tells people what she thinks of them and how they really smell. Furthermore, she refuses to kiss relatives or friends on command.

That particular day was like any other. Capri dropped her coat in the foyer, her backpack in the entrance of the den, and her artwork on the coffee table. She shunned her big girl persona and reverted to playing baby of the house: "Mommy, Mommy, I missed you, Mommy." Her thumb went into her mouth, and she climbed on top of me. We cuddled for a blissful moment. Her thumb got a brief reprieve.

"Mommy, I do not like dis weathuh."

"Me neither."

"Are you sick or sumthin'?"

"No, Mommy's just a little tired."

"Did you exacise or sumthin'?"

"No, I'm too old to exercise."

"How old are you anyway?"

"I'm thirty years old."

"No yaw not! Yaw fawty-one! Faker!"

"If you know my age, why did you ask?"

"I was just checkin' ta see if *you* know."

"Mommies know a lot of things."

"Will you be dead for my wedding?"

"No, I plan to be there. Daddy might be dead. He's older than me."

"How old will you be when I'm fawty?"

"I'll be seventy-five."

"How old will you be when I'm fifteen?"

"I'll be fifty." (Ouch)

"How will I find you when I get ta heaven?"

"I'll be in the Italian restaurant at the all-you-can-eat buffet."

"Mommy. I'm sewious."

"Oh, honey, you won't have to worry about that. Jesus will show you where I am."

"How does God put people in hell? Does he drop 'em in?"

"Well, no. It's kind of hard to explain but you don't need to worry because you're going to heaven."

"Does God have a list of who's goin' ta heaven?"

"Yes, as a matter of fact he does."

"What if yaw on da list and do a bad thing?"

"If you are really sorry for your sin, God can see into your heart and he will forgive you. The thief on the cross didn't act very nice, and he did a lot of bad things, but he is in heaven because he was very, very sorry and he believed in Jesus."

"Do we have ta brush teeth in heaven?"

"No, we'll all have dentures that don't wear out."

"Do we have ta take showuhs?"

"Nope. Everybody there smells good forever."

"I'm gonna like heaven. Just make shaw yaw right there when I get there."

She poked her tiny pointer finger close to my nose and said with rhythm, authority, and a semi-threatening tone, "Be at da gate and don't be late! You got it?"

I pulled her forty-pound frame closer toward me and held her tight. "I got it, babe. I got it."

PACIFIED

–Marilyn Meberg

At eighteen months old, my son, Jeff, was hopelessly addicted to his pacifier. This concerned me because he looked mildly moronic with that rubber plug perpetually hanging out of his mouth, and he smelled bad as well. The rubber literally began to rot from constant use, and the smell of its decay clung to Jeff wherever he went.

The obvious solution of providing a new pacifier didn't work because he flatly refused any contact with one. I thought, *Why on earth would anyone in their right mind refuse a brand-new, inoffensive pacifier when it provides a classier look and a better aroma?*

Clearly this child was not concerned with aesthetics. As the days dragged on, the odor intensified. I became desperate; my desperation produced tension. I studied Jeff as he would "plug in" his rank, little aid-to-peace, turning it slightly in his mouth until he achieved exactly the right feel. Then it hit me. He was attached to the old pacifier because it had ridges that conformed exactly to the contours of his mouth. It was a custom fit! It was familiar–homey– comfortable. The new one was foreign–sterile–stiff. At that moment I determined to form ridges on the new pacifier. There was only one way to do this–I would simply have to break it in myself!

I was well aware of the absurdity of this plan. The picture of a mother so driven by desperation that she would actually do what I was planning to do did amuse me. Nevertheless, in spite of the glimpse of humor I saw, I remained inordinately serious. I even entertained the possibility of Jeff and I developing a deeper level of camaraderie and identification as we went about each day sucking our mutual pacifiers.

On the first morning of this plan's enactment, Jeff settled in to watch *Captain Kangaroo*. As he plugged in, I sat down beside him and also plugged in. It took awhile for him to notice me, but when he did, he was vehement in his response. With a determined "NO!" he yanked the pacifier out of my mouth and threw it on the floor. This happened several times; each time I tried to explain that Jeff had his pacifier and Mommy had hers, and we were going to enjoy them together. (Incidentally, there is nothing enjoyable or even pacifying about sucking a pacifier. The little rubber center threatened to activate the gag impulse in me, my mouth became dry, and my lips tired from pooching out!) Jeff was unmoved by my explanation. Throughout the day, whenever Jeff saw it in my mouth, he would dash up to me, wrench it from my lips, and throw it on the floor. He skulked about the house in an attempt to catch me "at it." Since my plan distressed Jeff, I determined to take to the pacifier when he was safely put away.

That evening, shortly after Jeff had gone to bed, my husband, Ken, and I were sitting on the couch reading the paper. He made an interesting comment, and I lowered my paper in response. He exhibited the same shock and revulsion to my pacifier-stuffed mouth as Jeff had earlier. Later that night, when I thought Ken was asleep, I reached over to the nightstand and noiselessly slipped the pacifier in my mouth. After a few minutes Ken raised up on an elbow and demanded, "What's that munching sound?" I had no idea I was audibly munching. I was then informed that no man in his right mind would go to bed with a woman who slept with a pacifier.

The number of hours available to me for ridge-development were lessening all the time, but a workable pattern subsequently developed. I simply plugged in during Jeff's morning and afternoon naps, which gave me at least two hours a day to work on my project.

One morning about ten days later, I was vacuuming the living room, pacifier firmly in place. I thought I heard a knock. Without turning off the vacuum, I opened the door a few inches and peeked around it. To my chagrin there stood a salesman with a satchel full of brushes. As his face registered a look of complete bewilderment, I quickly unplugged both vacuum and pacifier. He had not said a word; he just stared. Seeing him back away, I felt compelled to explain what I was doing.

"Now wait a minute," I said. "I know this looks peculiar but, you see, this pacifier isn't mine! Well, what I mean is . . . it's my little boy's . . . he's asleep. It upsets him if I suck on it when he's awake. It upsets my husband too, for that matter! The only reason I've got this one in my mouth is because the other one got to smelling so bad I couldn't stand it any longer."

He continued staring at me. Just as I was about to launch into the importance of forming ridges and to show him that I was actually about to accomplish my goal, he burst into a fit of raucous laughter. He laughed, gasped, choked, and then laughed some more. I thought, *Well, really! I didn't invite this perfect stranger to my door . . . and now, having caught me at a rather awkward moment, he has the audacity to gasp and wheeze in the face of my explanations!* When he managed to get his breath, he raised one hand weakly in an almost defensive gesture and said, "Lady, I don't know what you are doing, and I don't care. I just want you to know you've made my day." He then went into another fit of laughter and lurched down the sidewalk toward his parked car. Strangely enough, I never saw that man again.

But whatever became of that pacifier? Several days later, without the slightest hesitation, Jeff took the pacifier I had broken in. Once again, a brave-hearted mother, determined to risk her own reputation, to say nothing of her dignity, for the sake of the child she loved, had gloriously prevailed! Funny, though, Jeff never quite saw it that way when I told him the story years later. Oh well, a mom's gotta do what she's gotta do, even if all the thanks she gets from her ungrateful child is: "Yuck!"

SCORCHED

—Nancy Coey

My friend tells this story about her two-year-old son:

He is very, very angry at her. Evidently she has offended him in some way and he wants to let her know just how mad he is. But he is having trouble because he knows very few words ... maybe twenty or so. He scrunches up his face; thrusts his head, turtle-like, from his neck, and seethes, "You, you ..."

But then he gets stuck.

He doesn't have a word for what he wants to say. You can see him thinking, making choices.

Finally he has it: "You, you ... firetruck!"

His mother jumps back, scorched.

Words can sometimes burn.

WHO'S THE BOSS?

−Carol Kent

My sister Joy and her four-year-old son, K.C., were eating a lunch of butter sandwiches when Joy decided to turn this mealtime into a teachable moment. She wanted to see what K.C.'s keen little mind could conjure up in response to a series of theological questions about authority and submission.

In between bites, she asked him simply, "Son, who is the boss of you?"

His voice sounded confident. "You, Mommy."

So far, so good. Her next question built on the first. "And who is the boss of Mommy?"

This question was not answered as swiftly as the first, but he finally managed to come up with a satisfactory answer. "Daddy," he replied, somewhat hesitantly.

"And who," she questioned, "is the boss of Daddy?"

She was searching for a very simple answer, indicating K.C. understood that God is our final authority. She wasn't expecting him to go up the authority ladder with responses like "church leadership" or "human government."

K.C. was struggling hard to come up with the correct answer. There was a definite question mark at the end of his answer. He replied, "Grandma and Grandpa?"

That answer was good enough to induce a chuckle from Joy.

However, a few hints later my nephew was able to come up with the response his mother was looking for–"God."

Joy couldn't stop there. She had one last question that would really tell her how her son was thinking. "Son, who will be the boss of you when you're a grownup?"

This question produced the greatest anxiety of all. K.C. took his time to ponder the question. Then, with great apprehension, he looked up with a furrowed brow and responded, "My wife?"

THE ART OF POTTY TRAINING

−Kathy Peel

*I*t's a miracle firstborn children grow up with any degree of emotional stability. They're the guinea pigs that must endure our trial-and-error methods of learning to mother.

One of the first crises every new mother encounters as her child grows from infant to preschooler is potty training. For me, this experience turned out to be about as joyous as dropping an iron on my foot. Every day of the process brought new challenges and tests of my endurance quotient.

I read that little girls mature earlier and are easier to potty train than little boys. Out to prove the experts wrong, I became a goal-driven woman. I was dead set on potty training John by his second birthday. Wrong-o.

There are three important points every mother needs to know as she begins to potty train her child. First, she needs to decide what terms she will use in the teaching process. Actually, after reading everything ever written on this topic and interviewing several experienced mothers, I learned there's a wide variety of opinions. Some approach potty training very seriously. To them, mothers who use terms such as "pee and poop," "go big potty," or "number one and number two" are foolish and irresponsible. Maybe I'm out of touch, but there's something about hearing a two year old say she needs to defecate that doesn't sit quite right (no pun intended). As for my own upbringing, I'm sure my mother's using the term "go shu-shu" has nothing to do with my need for a straitjacket.

With my children, I decided to go the initials route: "TT" and "BM." I don't think there's anything psychologically harmful about using these terms unless your preschooler cannot pronounce consonants clearly. In our case, "TT" worked fine, but "BM" came out—so to speak—"Mia" (pronounced mee-a). This can be very confusing to a babysitter or if your child is a guest at someone's house and walks around in circles repeating "Mia, Mia, Mia." They wonder if this is his grandmother's nickname or if he's been watching Italian movies. This term caused unnecessary trauma once on a family vacation when we stopped for the night at a motel called the Casa Mia. The kids cried because they thought we were spending the night in a big bathroom.

The second thing every mother needs to decide is what type of reward system she will use when the desired behavior occurs. I talked to mothers who kept candy jars in the bathroom and others who went so far as to offer a trip to the toy store for cooperation. But the prize for the strangest method goes to the mother who put her child's pet bird in the bathroom to give him some company while he sat. This gave new meaning to the term "stool pigeon."

I tried playing mood music, letting the faucet trickle, and promising to let John wear special Incredible Hulk underwear for a successful bathroom visit. I even bought a Tinkle Star potty chair that was supposed to play "Twinkle, Twinkle Little Star" upon victory. We never heard the song.

After months of frustration, I did what any mother in her right mind would have done. I threw in the towel and simply gave up the fight. Shortly afterward, my firstborn child, my guinea pig, John, simply potty trained himself!

BODY SNATCHERS

–Karen M. Leet

I felt like running through the streets warning people: "They're coming! They're coming! Run for your lives," I would scream. But no one would hear me. No one would respond. It was like one of those horrible dreams in which you try and try to scream, but nothing comes out. Or a dream in which you try to run for your life, but the air is too thick to breathe and the stuff under your feet is thick, gluey muck.

In my saner moments, when my brain agreed to function for a flash, I recalled a scene, I think, from an old black-and-white movie, *Invasion of the Body Snatchers*.

A grim-faced little boy stubbornly insists that his mom isn't his mom anymore. Or was it a little girl? Anyway, the child is utterly convinced that the person seeming to be a nice, normal mom is a fake, a bogus mom. Of course, no one believed the child. No one ever believes the first sign of disaster.

But this was a disaster of at least equal proportions. My child had disappeared. I don't mean he had been kidnapped or anything like that. Though in my worst moments, I'm tempted to call a kidnappers' agency or whatever and leave my address.

No, I don't really mean that. At least I don't think I do. No, of course I don't. My child had disappeared. One night I tucked him in, kissed his soft, downy cheek, read his favorite Bible story, prayed with him, smiled to hear his God-blesses, and hugged him tight (because sometimes I get an urge to hug him the way we hugged when he was little, when we called them "bonecrunchers").

Then I switched off the light and hurried to collect the jeans from the dryer. That was the last time I saw my son.

"Where are my jeans?" demanded the person who rose from my son's bed.

"I beg your pardon?"

"Where are my jeans? I only have one pair that fit right, and they're not in my drawer," growled the intruder whose light brown hair curled against his temples exactly the way my son's did.

"I put some more in the dryer last night. You could check down there," I murmured, stunned almost speechless. Where was my son? Who was this rude and surly stranger, stalking from room to room criticizing everything in his path?

"Isn't there anything to eat around here? Where's my math homework? I left it right here on the table. Don't touch that book. It's mine."

His younger brother stared up from his cereal bowl. His mouth fell open. Crisp and Crunchy Something-or-others dribbled down his chin.

"Can't you make him stop that?" demanded the creature swabbing up juice with a hunk of toast, dripping milk across the table, scattering crumbs freely on a rumpled, torn, and grubby shirt. "He's disgusting!"

I clutched for self-control. Disgusting? The little brother who admired and imitated him? The little brother who followed him around the house and who applauded when he hit a pop fly? The little brother who struggled to comb his hair the same way and even tried to wear similar clothes?

That's when I knew. This was an alien life form, a pod person, some horrible beast from another world that had cleverly disguised itself in my son's shape.

It might fool his friends, the neighbors, even his grandparents, but it wouldn't fool me. It might wear the same clothes, though they often looked as if they'd ripened under the bed for a week, and I think they usually had. It might wear its hair in the same style

154

and have the same color eyes, though I had trouble being sure about eye color. Hair screened it from view much of the time.

It might eat the same favorite foods, though in far greater quantity. I never knew one entity—I won't say person—could consume so much food at one time and still walk away upright. Do aliens have a higher metabolism or what?

It might sleep in my son's room and know my son's favorite color and where I hide the chocolate mints. It might flash a familiar dimple at me when it forgets to be rude and obnoxious long enough to laugh at an old joke. It might even know my son's favorite Bible story and best baseball card and pet name for the family guinea pig.

But this was not my son. My son laughed a lot. My son rushed to help me carry out laundry to the clothesline. My son fit into the family like a finger in a glove. My son admired his dad, protected his brother, hugged his mom. My son wrote notes to tell us how much he loved us and taped them on the refrigerator.

My son adored church, could hardly wait for Sunday mornings, and even liked dressing up in his sports jacket and tie. My son knew dozens of Bible verses, tried his best to tell the truth and obey God, and struggled to be kind to people who weren't kind to him.

My son slept with a half smile on his face, not a sneer. He was eager and open about his feelings. He did well in school, and though he never actually admitted it, he enjoyed his teachers and didn't mind the work even when it was a struggle for him.

I wonder where the formless pod was stashed that night when the invaders snatched my son away? I'm glad I didn't witness the transformation. I know it's a genuine invasion too. Friends and neighbors are beginning to suspect that their own sons and daughters have been replaced by alien beings.

I've seen the puzzled faces as loving parents peer into familiar features wondering, "Can this be my child?" They're catching on. The pod people won't win this one.

We're going to fight. They're not going to take over the world. I might organize some moms from church to track down those body-snatching aliens. I'll definitely be praying and asking God for help.

I want my son back, and I believe I'll get him. It might take time. I'm sure it will take prayer and patience and the sort of love God specializes in—the kind that never gives up, doesn't take offense, and keeps on forgiving. I don't think it will be easy.

"Hey, isn't anybody ever going to fix any dinner around here?"

"Casserole's in the oven. I have a loaf of bread to hold you till it's done." I will never give up. I will never stop praying and caring and doing everything I know how to do to get my son back. The pod people are going to lose this one, and that's a fact.

Chapter Eight

Laughter: The Glue That Holds Friendships Together

Laughter is the shortest distance between two people.

—Victor Borge

FRIENDSHIP BREAD

—Liz Curtis Higgs

$\mathcal{A}$lthough I spent the first two dozen years of my life in Lancaster County, Pennsylvania, I had never heard of Amish Friendship Bread. One day a friend brought me a small loaf of it, and I was hooked. "Do you want some 'starter'?" she asked. Even though it sounded to me like something you put in your car, I said, "Sure!"

She showed up the next day with a bag of glop and a recipe that had obviously been photocopied dozens of times. The instructions were very clear: "*Do not* use metal spoon or bowl when mixing! *Do not* refrigerate! *Expel air* from bag occasionally." Then this ominous note: "It is normal for batter to thicken, bubble, and ferment." And they want me to eat this? Too late. I'd already eaten it.

"Okay, what do I do first?" I asked her.

"Nothing."

"You mean you just set it on the counter?"

"Right. And *do not* refrigerate!"

Got that. "What about tomorrow?"

"Squeeze it."

"You gotta be kidding!"

"Read the recipe. Days Two, Three, Four, and Five it just says, 'Squeeze Bag.'"

Now, this is my kind of baking. Day Six you have to open the bag and add some flour, sugar, and milk. But no fridge. Yuck. Three more days of squeezing, then the contents of the bag move to a big bowl. More flour, sugar, and milk. Then—here's where starter is born—you divide the glop evenly into four Ziploc bags and give three of them to friends.

I am doomed! I do not have three friends who cook! Bill, however, is elated at the thought of taking bags of glop to work and carries three off Monday morning with fresh photocopies of the infamous recipe. Finally, it's time to get serious about turning the glop into bread. I pour the fourth bag of glop into a bowl—not metal!—and stir in oil, vanilla, eggs, and baking power. That's not a typo, that's what the recipe said I needed: "1-1/2 teaspoons of Baking Power." Heaven knows, I've needed that for years.

More ingredients are added, including "1 Large Box Vanilla Pudding." One wonders how big they made boxes of pudding when this recipe was first written. At the discount shopping clubs, you can now buy one box of pudding that will feed an entire Middle School. I guess at how large they mean "Large" to be, dump the batter into two pans that have been sugared (not floured), and bake for one hour.

The problem is, you have now baked your starter and you are left with nothing to squeeze for the next ten days, until Friends One, Two, and Three all give you back a new bag of starter (actually, your own starter in another life—hard to believe the Amish would go for reincarnation like this). In theory, the Friendship Bread I'm eating today could have molecules of the original starter from, say, Noah's mother. Imagine: centuries of starter, from Joan of Arc to Joan Baez, all in my mixing bowl. Maybe this is what Mother meant when she said, "Don't touch that! You never know where it's been."

A new, more immediate concern comes into view. Let's say you have a bag of three-day-old starter, plus another one from last week, and a third bag of glop walks in the door. It could take a separate calendar just to keep track of which one to squeeze when or who needed stirring (do not use metal spoon). Or what if someone accidentally made their bread on Day Nine? Would it hold their oven hostage for twenty-four hours? Or worse, what if you don't get around to tossing the Baking Power in there until Day Twelve? Will the bowl become a small nuclear device?

With a sigh of relief, I get to the final note at the bottom of the recipe: "This bread is forgiving." (Thanks, I needed that.) "If you miss a few days, just squeeze daily until you can bake it." It sounds so heartless, until I realize that's the same method I've used to keep my family happy for the last nine years: a quick squeeze, a kiss on the cheek, an "I promise we'll have more time together soon!" and I'm off to play in other kitchens.

My Amish neighbors may be on to something. Time to bring home my flour from afar and bake some bread. First, I need a friend with starter ...

STORMY WEATHER

—Thelma Wells

*S*ometimes you don't realize how great your friends are until your world starts rocking. That's what happened to me on April 17, 1998, in Nashville, Tennessee. So many tornadoes came to town that day it's a wonder I can still think straight to tell the story. You may recall the news reports of the wreckage they left behind, but you certainly won't remember reading how Thelma Wells had just settled down for an afternoon nap on the twenty-fifth floor of her hotel at the precise moment the tornadoes went roaring by.

There I was, skirt off, snuggled comfortably into my terry cloth hotel robe, badly in need of a rest before my evening speaking engagement. Then I heard it. A rumbling like a train coming full speed ahead. But I was halfway to heaven in that tall hotel room. How could I hear a train way up on the twenty-fifth floor of an air-conditioned hotel?

"What's that?" I yelled to Pat, my friend and traveling companion.

Her eyes were as wide as mine as we watched part of the hotel break loose and come flying past the window. For a moment, we froze, like startled children who'd just seen a cow jump over the moon.

Then we ran for cover. I hurried to the bathroom, trying to cram myself under the sink, like a frightened chipmunk scrambling for its hole.

"Fool, get out from under there," Pat's sensible voice scolded me. "That sink will fall on you and you'll be just a greasy spot on the floor. Are you crazy!"

But then the building started swaying from side to side, jostling us as though we were mere bits of clothing in a washing machine that had suddenly gone off balance.

A terrified voice shouted over the hotel's loudspeakers: "This is not a drill! This is not a drill! [Imagine staging a drill like this!] We are having a tornado. Get downstairs immediately. Do not use the elevators. Get to the ballroom immediately and take cover. Use the stairs."

I may have been scared out of my wits, but I knew one thing— I wasn't about to go anywhere without my skirt, shoes, purse, and Bible (fortunately I had my blouse on under my robe). After all, I could hardly show up at my speaking engagement dressed for bed. So I pulled my skirt half on and scooted toward the stairwell.

As Pat and I reached the stairs, people hurried past us. Some were going so fast they rushed right out of their shoes. Others took flying leaps, skipping over several steps at once in their haste to reach the ballroom before the building fell over. My goals were simpler. I just wanted to hold onto everything and keep my robe closed so I wouldn't flash anybody on the way down.

But nobody was paying any attention to me. Instead, they were dashing, running, smashing, leaping, hollering, and cursing. By the eleventh floor I'd had enough. The truth is I could hardly breathe by then, my asthma was so bad.

"Go on down," I ordered Pat. "Save your life. I'm going to die right here on the eleventh floor. If I'm blown away, they can put a plaque up as a memorial. You go on down and save yourself."

Pat wouldn't hear of it. "You must be crazy, Thelma. I'm not moving until you do. Come on, you can make it."

Trouble was I didn't want to make it. I was comfortable with my decision to crumble right then and there. But three big guys noticed I was having a hard time and offered to carry me the rest of the way.

"Listen, honey," I told them, "you'll get hernias and be unable to have kids if you carry me down. No way I'm going to deprive some poor child of his daddy."

After a few more minutes I decided I could breathe after all, at least enough to save Pat's life. When we finally limped into the ballroom, legs quivering, we were the last ones in. By then we had seen the worst of the tornadoes.

For the next three days, however, I was so bent over I could hardly walk. Muscles I didn't even know I had screamed at me day and night, scolding me for treating them so badly. During the weekend conference, lights had to be dimmed for my entrance onto the stage so that I could preserve at least a shred of dignity. But as I stiffed it to the middle of the platform, I couldn't help but smile just a little.

Pat, my tried and true friend, had refused to leave my side when I thought I couldn't possibly move another step. She had scolded me and encouraged me until I was able to make the rest of the journey to safety. What a friend! Just like Ruth was to Naomi, refusing to leave even though the circumstances looked awful (of course, I'm not nearly as old as Naomi and Pat not nearly as young as Ruth). Who knows what would have happened if my good friend hadn't stood by me. Why, I might still be huddled like a poor little chipmunk under the sink in my room on the twenty-fifth floor!

SHADES
OF LUCY
AND ETHEL

−Luci Swindoll

$\mathcal{O}$ne day my dear, zany friend, Marilyn Meberg, and I began to chat about her next speaking engagement, which was to occur on a Saturday at a nearby restaurant. Since she is one of my favorite speakers, I asked if I might tag along just to keep her company and to benefit once again from her speaking prowess. But Marilyn was sure I would be bored since she was giving a talk I had already heard more than once.

But I kept insisting. Before long, we were entertaining various ideas for how to spice things up. I would attend the meeting in disguise or with a peculiarity that only she would know about, just for fun, just to see if I could pull it off. And all the while we were laughing heartily at all the absurdities that might unfold if were I brave enough to play the part.

Then suddenly Marilyn decided to issue a real challenge. Knowing full well that ridiculous contests are one of my favorite forms of recreation, she outlined the details of her challenge, promising a rich reward if I would agree. "Luci," she said, "I will take you to the Hobbit Restaurant as my guest, if you will do the following on Saturday at the women's luncheon where I'm speaking ..."

Now, wait a minute! Before I tell you the requirements for my prize, let me acquaint you with the Hobbit, a restaurant to which I had never been but had longed to go. The Hobbit is an exceptional establishment in every sense of the word. It offers a one-sitting-per-evening, multi-course, set-price dining experience without equal in Southern California. Reservations are required months in advance. The evening begins promptly at 7:30 P.M., when the guests meet in the wine cellar for half an hour of hors d'oeuvres, champagne, and conversation. At eight o'clock, everyone moves upstairs to the dining area for a seven-course dinner, interrupted halfway through to visit the Hobbit Gallery, an exhibit of fine art. Every guest has the same menu, which changes weekly and is rarely repeated. Men are to dress in coat and tie, women in long skirts. Very elegant!

Sound fun? Sound delicious? Sound unique? Well, my friends, it is all of that ... and more. And to think, I could have it all without spending one red cent. But—and here's the catch—were I to fulfill Marilyn's demands, the payment for such an evening would cost me in self-respect. This was her proposal:

"Luci, you must come to the luncheon in a dress and dark glasses."

I thought, "All right! No problem."

"And Luci, you must stay at least thirty minutes."

Again, "No problem, Marilyn—thirty minutes out of a Saturday is a piece of cake ... so what's the deal?"

Then, "You must wear your Mobil hard hat [I was working for Mobil Oil at the time], and when spoken to, respond with a speech impediment! And you have to act totally unaware of your strange appearance, as though you feel perfectly at ease and at home dressed and speaking in that manner."

Suddenly the Hobbit, in all its succulent fantasy, receded into the regions of never-never land, replaced in my imagination by an apparition of Luci Swindoll in dark glasses, a dress, and Mobil hard hat, talking with a pronounced speech impediment to a luncheon filled with sedate, respectable Christian women. I couldn't do it. I simply could not consent to sacrificing my dignity, even for the most delectable meal on earth. Marilyn left that day with one final dangling of the bait—"Remember. You've always wanted to eat at the Hobbit. You'll never have a better offer." Then she closed the door and walked away.

When Saturday rolled around, I was recalling our idiotic bet as I was finishing my morning chores. Suddenly, without the slightest provocation, a little voice inside my head said, "Do it."

I stopped dead in my tracks and said out loud, "What?"

"Do it, Luci. Don your hard hat and hit that meeting. Think of the fun you'd have.... And Marilyn? Well, she'll drop her teeth. She's so wacky, she's probably forgotten about the bet altogether. Imagine the look on her face when she sees you standing in that room, dressed as she prescribed, acting as though you belong there. She'll die. And you'll be the winner—you can relive it over and over again for the rest of your life. Dinner at the Hobbit! Do it!"

Taking it as the voice of the Holy Spirit, I began to get dressed. By this time I was so jazzed I could hardly wait to make my entrance. Quickly I put on a navy blue dress (to match the Mobil emblazoned on my hard hat) and a pair of dressy heels, grabbed my briefcase, and tore out to the meeting. Just before I walked into the luncheon, I placed the hard hat firmly on my head, tilting it slightly to the right and tossing a piece of chewing gum in my mouth for good measure. Then I strolled in.

Inside the door, a number of models were milling about. They were part of a style show designed to delight the fashionable, well-coifed women who had gathered to enjoy a lovely lunch—about two hundred women in all. At first no one paid any attention to me or my ridiculous getup. Perhaps they thought I was modeling the latest in hard hat fashions!

But Marilyn, from her perch at the head table, spotted me the minute I entered. The look on her face was priceless. Have you ever seen someone who looked as though they had just been goosed by an electric prod (one of Marilyn's favorite images)? Well, that's the way she looked. Shocked. Stunned. Confused.

Although I was screaming with laughter inside, I went right on calmly chewing my gum. The style-show ladies seemed irritated as they walked around me, lining up for their part of the program. But I never budged, standing right in the middle of the entrance, with cocked hat, pretty dress, dark glasses, and briefcase.

Finally a lady from the head table approached and asked if there was anything she could do to help me. "Oh, no thank you," I answered with an impeded nasal twang. "I'm fine." Looking a bit baffled, the lady returned to the head table, which by now was abuzz with what the Bible refers to as "murmurings and disputings." I began to read lips—"Who is she?" "What does she want?" "Is she some kind of official?"

During all this, Marilyn's face could have won an Academy Award. Every second brought a new expression, ranging from strained control to near collapse. She was marvelous, and before I knew it I was having the time of my life. When the fashion show was over, before the special music began, I walked into the room and leaned against the back wall, strategically placing myself in full view of the head table, doing my best to look both weird and official.

Those poor women; bless their innocent hearts. They didn't know what to do. Every once in a while they would cast curious glances in my direction but would look away whenever they caught my eye. It was the most collectively baffled look I have ever had the pleasure of witnessing. When the singer performed, I took off my hard hat and piously covered my heart. As the announcements were given, I took copious notes. In short, I entered in fully, just as the challenge required, and never once blew my cover. But the funniest part was yet to come.

After several failed attempts from various women to ascertain my true identity and purpose, I began to hear the strains of a victory march playing triumphantly in my heart. "Oh, Hobbit, here we come!" I caught Marilyn's eye, mouthing to her that my thirty minutes time limit was up and I was going home. But just then, she was introduced as the speaker. Quickly, she motioned for me to stay. So I leaned back against the wall and obeyed. By now I had won anyway.

Marilyn drew herself up behind the podium. "Ladies, before I begin," she said, "I have been tremendously curious about that roving lady in the Mobil hard hat. Have you?" Everyone, en masse, turned around and looked straight at me. I nodded with a slight smile. She went on, gesturing toward me, "Is there anything we can do for you or is there a question that perhaps we could answer?"

With all the dignity I could muster, I stepped forward, and in a loud, pronouncedly defective voice I announced to the mesmerized audience that I was with Mobil Oil Corporation, and we were going to be digging a trench in front of the building momentarily. Some of their cars were in the way and would have to be moved. The digging crew was waiting for my signal to begin. Since the speaker looked rather longwinded, however, I had intended to wait until she had finished before calling out a list of license numbers of cars that would be affected. Then I read some fictitious license numbers I had already written on the back of a card.

Marilyn could stand it no longer. She lost her breath laughing. While many of the other women joined her (those who had been secretly giggling the whole time), others looked worried, either wondering what their license numbers were or else fearing my feelings would be hurt if it seemed they were laughing at my unfortunate speech impediment. After a bit, Marilyn gathered herself together and introduced me for real, explaining our ludicrous bet and how she never in a million years expected me to take her up on the challenge. "But I have found out Luci will do anything for a free meal," she said, still laughing. There was a slight pause, then everyone broke into enthusiastic applause as I gave the *Rocky* victory sign. In my normal voice, I thanked them all for being so very gracious about the whole thing and assured them that their cars were quite safe. Smiling to the group, I turned around and walked out. As the door closed behind me, the sound of their continued applause and laughter rang in my ears. Such a nice sound.

Eight months later, the evening at the Hobbit became a reality. It was all we had anticipated—just great! Marilyn once again acknowledged her utter surprise at my bravery and ability to allow my dignity to be reduced by such daring and fearless behavior. "Well, Marilyn," I said, "what are friends for, anyway?"

WAX BUILDUP, ANTHROPOLOGY, AND STARCHED PILLOWCASES

–Sue Buchanan

*T*he first time I remember making a conscientious effort to cultivate friends was when Wayne and I were first married. We lived in a tiny fourth-floor walkup apartment in an industrial section of Chicago. We commuted two hours a day to and from the city to our daytime jobs. To supplement our income, Wayne was music director, and I was his accompanist, in a small church.

Our apartment would be called delightful, even darling, by today's standards. That was before we learned to appreciate ancient buildings with hardwood floors, thick plaster walls, and fourteen-foot ceilings with triple-crown molding.

It never occurred to us to turn the ugly, black fire escape outside our kitchen window into a balcony of beauty by adding pots of pansies and geraniums, or into a ledge of usefulness with an herb garden of parsley and oregano.

We were anxious to make friends in those days. We often managed to pack the whole church choir into our three-room apartment for a party, and once in a great while, we could save enough money for an evening in the city with others from the young adult Sunday school class. These were times of raucous laughter and fun, but it wasn't the same as having close couple friends–people with whom we could savor a good meal and more importantly, enjoy lively conversation.

169

I'll never forget the first couple we entertained. The conversation never veered from one topic. *Cleaning.* Cleaning, as in cleaning our scroungy little apartments. "What did you guys do today?" I asked as we sat down to dinner. Since I asked the leading question, I suppose you could say it was my fault that for the next three hours we discussed such things as the cause of wax buildup and how to rid ourselves of this pesky blight. *Steel wool? Razor blades? Ajax? Bon-Ami? Or perhaps some miracle-working commercial product yet to be discovered?*

"Do you iron your sheets? Do you starch your pillowcases? Do you carry your garbage down to the alley every day or every other day?"

"Do you change your dishwater before you scour your pots and pans?" They did! And they said so vehemently! And they had some pretty disparaging remarks about people who didn't! When all eyes turned to me, I certainly wasn't going to admit to being one of those people.

"It's like adding grease to grease," I said. "I not only run fresh water—hot, hot water—I double the soap!" Now I'm not proud of this—because it was all a huge lie—but I then wrinkled up my nose, leaned across the table, and said in a voice barely above a whisper, that I couldn't possibly cook my next meal in pans with a grease residue as thick as the grease on Elvis's pompadour.

A few weeks later Wayne suggested we try again and invite another couple for dinner. We hardly knew Ernie and Barb. They came to church only on special occasions, probably to please Ernie's parents who never missed a service. They sat reverently on the side next to the organ—Ernie's mother was the organist—with tolerant little smiles that made me think they knew something the rest of us didn't. They were getting advance degrees. In the words of Ernie's mother, they were both "smart as a crack, and working night and day on their doctors [sic]." Down deep I thought perhaps some of their "smart as a crack" would rub off on us and at the very least, the dinner conversation would be more stimulating than it was with Mr. and Mrs. Grease Residue.

On the appointed evening, I cooked a big pot of spaghetti, which was all we could afford at the time, and tossed a salad. Wayne sliced the French bread and adjusted the HiFi (before stereo). My Formica-topped table looked elegant in the candlelight, set perfectly with my new wedding china and crystal.

"Nice apartment," Ernie muttered as he looked around. "We could never invite friends over. We have books stacked everywhere. Every table. Every chair. Barely a path to the bathroom."

"Nice table," Barb commented. "China and crystal are such a bother. In fact, ours is stored, and it will be stored till we're out of graduate school. Perhaps longer. It'll be years before we have time to entertain." This last statement caused me to rule out the fact that we might receive a reciprocal invitation any time soon.

Within the first five minutes we learned that our guests were not taking the easy way out (they told us this) when it came to their education. Both were majoring in anthropology.

For the life of me I couldn't remember a thing about anthropology except for some lyrics to a Smothers Brothers song that said, "My old man's an anthropologist, now whattaya think about that? He wears an anthropologist raincoat and an anthropologist hat." I knew Wayne was thinking the same thing, and I saw his mouth drop open in disbelief when, in my most polite voice, I asked, "Exactly what does an anthropologist do?" (I knew! I just couldn't recall at the moment.)

Eventually we managed to turn the topic of conversation to the subject of friendship, which was, in fact, the very reason for inviting Ernie Jr. and Barb to dinner in the first place. Apparently, they too had tried to establish relationships with other couples and had struck out.

"Tom and Beth?" Barb said. "Nothing in common. *They* major in music!"

Ernie's turn. "Alex and Jane?" Again nothing in common. "They have a *baby*. We can't even *think* baby at this point."

"Earl and Jessie? Into sports!" *Worse than being into the occult!* was implied by the tone in Barb's voice.

"We thought we had something going with Paul and Ann," Barb continued wistfully. "They're in school too, both in doctoral programs, but you know what the problem is? We're majoring in different things. Totally different interests!"

At last, we said our good-byes with no empty "let's-do-it-again" promises. Wayne and I headed for the kitchen.

"Wonder what they'll say about us? 'That poor Buchanan woman didn't even know what anthropology is!'"

"As you can see, I'm up to my elbows here in the reality of human behavior as it applies to the physical, social, and cultural development of human behavior as it applies to the physical, social, and cultural development of man," Wayne said in mock seriousness, as he scoured a saucepan in the much too greasy dishwater.

"Right," I responded, holding a wet dishrag in hand. "This is a hands-on, scientific interpretation of reality in light of human values and experience."

We bantered on, "Let me ask you a question, a question that could determine how we interpret the reality of the universe as a marital unit." By now the last dish was put away, and I was exaggerating my words and teasing my husband, through the living room and down the hall. "Exactly, what is your point of view when it comes to the ironing and starching of sheets and pillowcases? Because when all is said and done, I'm not at all sure that you and I—the two of us—have anything in common whatsoever."

With that I took a flying leap into the middle of the bed, and he was right behind me.

"I think we do!" he answered. "I think we do!"

Chapter Nine

Chortles from Church

He that believes in him shall have ever-laughing life.

—Anonymous

"SSSHHH! YOU'RE IN CHURCH!"

*I*n my pastor's opening remarks last Sunday, he said that every day is a new day: "We all make decisions from the moment we get up. We decide whether to have breakfast or not. We decide what shoes to wear. We decide whether to wear pants or a skirt—well, women can decide that anyway—because most men don't wear skirts ... at least those who belong to this church ... I hope. I, uh, probably should continue with my sermon before I get in more trouble."

—D. M., Arizona

The lesson topic was earthly possessions and how we put too much value on them. My husband was listing some of these possessions, such as money, fancy homes, recreational toys, and even living possessions such as pets. He said, "Yes, even our pets can sometimes have more value than they should. But what am I talking about, when I sleep with a dog!" Suddenly there was a heavy silence. He thought to himself, *I wonder if anyone thinks I was referring to my wife?* He cautiously looked across the room and there were a couple of people holding in explosive laughs. He quickly said, "No, no, I don't mean my wife. I mean Jo Jo, our dog!" Too late.

—G. O., Montana

As an usher passing the collection plate one Sunday, I waited while a couple who had given their daughter a dime struggled to get her to let go of it. As they pried it from her fingers, she angrily yelled, "I don't see why I have to pay anything, I didn't want to come here anyway!"

–R. B., Vermont

At a ladies' prayer meeting, I asked God for a car to replace the "lemon" we were using.

A week later, my parents came to visit, and let me borrow their Lincoln Town Car. As I pulled into the church parking lot, my amazed friends remembered my request from the previous week.

"Hey!" one woman exclaimed. "Our daughter needs a car for college. Let's pray for her!"

–Sue Shoger

PRAISE YE THE LORD!

−Patsy Clairmont

My niece, Susan, assisted with a singing group at her church. Called the Music Sprouts, the singers were three and four year olds. The song they learned was "Praise Ye the Lord." Gratefully, it was a song of few words and constant repetitions, making it easier for everyone to memorize. After practice one evening, Susan heard a little sprout practicing her lines as she left the church. In her clearest voice she sang, "Crazy the Lord, hallelujah! Crazy the Lord, hallelujah!"

Sometimes when I'm not certain what the Lord is doing, I sing that same song. The Lord is unpredictable; you can almost predict it. I guess it's not so important for us to be certain of what or how the Lord will perform his will, but just to be certain he will. But sometimes it's difficult to believe the best when you feel you are the worst. In my twenties, I was not only an agoraphobic, but I was also addicted to tranquilizers, caffeine, and nicotine. I smoked two packs of cigarettes a day for years. After becoming a believer, I wanted to quit, but my addiction was so strong, and I was weak. I repeatedly asked the Lord to deliver me, but it wasn't happening.

Then there came a voice from heaven. No, it wasn't the angel of the Lord, but it was nonetheless an angel (unaware). My Jewish friend, Louie, said to me, "You're using all your strength to give up smoking. Don't worry about the cigarettes. Instead, take that strength and use it to fall more deeply in love with Jesus, and one day the cigarettes will give *you* up."

Following my talk with Louie, I attended Bible studies, church, and women's retreats, nurturing my love for Jesus. Then it happened . . . I was certain it was time. I was at a friend's house, and I told Rose the cigarettes were ready to give me up. She called to Daryl, another friend, to join us in the kitchen. Rose then announced that we would pray, but first we would anoint me with oil. She checked her cupboard and found she was out of oil. "Not to worry," Rose said, because she had a can of Crisco. She scooped out a dollop on her finger and splatted it onto my forehead. (Do you know what happens when Crisco meets body heat?) I felt like a French fry. Rose then offered to lead the prayer. My thought was, *Good. While she prays, I'll dab the Crisco from my drippy eyebrows.* Then she and Daryl placed their hands on my shoulders and prayed. And I never smoked again. Praise Ye the Lord!

The next time you discover certitude has turned into uncertainty, you might try humming a few bars of "Crazy the Lord." It will remind you that what at first crazes us can turn into praises to him. Of that you can be certain.

YOUR CHICKENS WILL COME HOME TO ROOST

–Susan Duke

*O*ne of my mother's favorite maxims was "Your chickens will come home to roost," often followed by "you mark my words, Suzie, one day they will!" And one day they did. Although I'm not proud of it, I must admit, on occasion I'd embarrass my mother in public. It was usually in an innocent, humorous way, but it still left my mother red-faced and flustered. Like the Sunday–I was about four years old–when suddenly I was filled with the urge to belt out a song with the rest of the congregation. While the others softly sang, "Amazing Grace," I climbed boldly atop the church pew and sang a song my older brother had taught me–"Hey Joe, Where'd You Get That Pretty Girlie?" My brother, who couldn't contain his outburst of laughter, had to be led outside by our aggravated Mama.

Strange how this particular chicken "came home to roost" years later while sitting in a Wednesday evening church service with my own daughter, Kelly.

Midweek service was generally reserved for a time of prayer. Kelly, a junior in high school at the time, was normally quiet and reserved in the church setting. As the pastor asked for those who had a prayer request to raise their hand, I watched curiously as

Kelly lifted hers and waited for her turn to speak. When called upon, she earnestly offered her request.

"I would like to ask everyone to pray for a friend of mine who is really going through a rough time. She is going into the hospital tomorrow morning to have a vasectomy."

For a moment there was nothing but stunned silence. When it became obvious that I, the mother, had been silently elected to correct my daughter's indiscretion, I very gently took her hand and said, "Honey, you mean hysterectomy."

My normally quiet daughter, raised her voice and sharply retorted, "No, Mother, I mean vasectomy!"

Again, as demurely as possible, I repeated my previous statement, tagging on an extra clarification. "Sweetheart, men have vasectomies and women have hysterectomies." Convinced this would halt any further discussion, Kelly unpredictably turned downright indignant. She insisted she knew exactly what she was talking about. Snickers, held in restraint, now burst forth helplessly from all over the church. Red-faced and fighting to keep his composure, our pastor proposed, "Well, whatever the problem, we know we need to pray. Let's all kneel at our seats and bring these requests before the Lord."

At that point the laughter came roaring down the aisles like Niagara Falls, washing away any hope of saving grace. Out-and-out hysteria reigned. As I caught glimpses of others on their knees, shaking, bobbing, snorting, hee-hawing, and wiping away tears, my own embarrassment gave way to bellows of laughter. The pastor couldn't pray, and the church sounded like a barn full of braying donkeys. Why, if anyone had walked in at that moment, they'd have thought revival had broken out.

Though church was cut short that evening, we all left with our prescriptions filled by the good medicine of laughter. Instead of bowing our heads and folding our hands quietly in prayer, we had been so tickled that we had nearly fallen out of our pews—all because a bunch of chickens had finally come home to roost, just like Mama said they would!

ANTICS

—Marilyn Meberg

*S*everal years ago, my dear friend, Luci Swindoll, and I unintentionally threw a local pastor into a zany situation. Ken was on a business trip, and in his absence, I convinced Luci to accompany me on a Sunday morning visit to a church in our area. Neither of us had ever attended the church before.

We entered the small but cozy sanctuary and were seated by a friendly usher who handed us visitor cards and whispered that they would be picked up shortly. I didn't want to fill in the requested information because I knew I would not be returning. Not wanting to appear ungracious, however, I whispered to Luci that I was going to turn in the card but with a name other than my own and an out-of-state address so the visitation committee would know I was just "Passing through." Luci nodded and said she would do the same.

I wrote my mother's name and the address from Vancouver, Washington, where I had grown up and handed the card back to the waiting usher. Luci, before handing her card over, quickly showed me what she had written: "Miss Bernadette Apes"—with my address and phone number. I stifled a combination groan and giggle as she handed her card to the usher.

At the conclusion of the service, to my absolute horror, the pastor said, "Now, here's my favorite part of the service—the introducing of our visitors to the congregation." When he came to my card, in a stack of about fifteen, he said, "Elizabeth Ricker?" I raised my hand. "I see you're from Vancouver, Washington."

"Ah . . . yes, yes, I am."

"Well, Washington is a lovely, green state—what a beautiful place to live. I hope you'll enjoy visiting California as much as I always enjoy visiting Washington."

I nodded in weak response as he reached for the next card. He held it for just a moment in an attempt to comprehend the name.

"Uh . . . Bernadette Apes. Miss . . . Bernadette Apes? Are you here somewhere Miss Apes?"

Luci soberly raised her hand. I was biting the inside of my lip to the point of bleeding as he attempted a brief exchange with the shy, retiring Miss Apes. She assured the pastor she was a long-term resident of Fullerton and that she was a lonely person. I nearly exploded inside with laughter. I thought, *Luci—you moron—how on earth can you do the crazy things you do, especially in the name of my address and phone number?* At the conclusion of the service, we made a hasty escape to the parking lot and fell over the hood of my car in hysterics.

The following Tuesday night Ken responded to a knock on the front door. A man whom Ken did not know said, "Could I please speak with Bernadette Apes?"

"Pardon me?" (Ken had not heard about our escapade.)

"Miss Bernadette Apes . . . may I speak with her please?"

"Well, I'm sorry, but there must be some mistake . . ."

The man held up the visitor card and asked if he was at the correct address. Ken said that the address was right, but the person was not. The man apologized and left.

After explaining the whole incident to my long-suffering husband, I was overcome with a sense of guilt and concern for the poor man who had come to our house. I was sure he had given up a relaxing evening at home to embark on a fruitless search for Miss Apes.

The next day I phoned the pastor of the church, identified myself, and confessed the whole incident. In the midst of my profuse apologizing, he emitted a beautifully rich, baritone laugh that increased in intensity until he could hardly breathe. I wanted to hug him. When he got his breath he say, "Marilyn, my wife and I went out for dinner after the service and just roared over that incident. I described to her the masterful control I exhibited in reading Miss Bernadette Apes's name and then my feelings as I attempted to talk with her. I wondered if the whole thing were on the level, but I had to keep my composure in case it were. I can't wait to tell my wife about your call."

Here's a man who saw the humor in the antics of two women during an otherwise normal Sunday service. He could have chosen to fret internally over the unexpected appearance of Miss Apes's name on the visitor card and then reprimand me for the incident because it threatened to make him lose his dignity and possibly disrupt the service. Instead, he chose to laugh. The following Christmas I received a card from this wonderful pastor and his wife addressed to "Miss Bernadette Apes" and signed, "Still smiling."

My Mother, My Self–Eeek!

It is quite surprising how many children survive in spite of their mothers.

—Norman Douglas

Our mothers always remain the strangest, craziest people we've ever met.

—Marguerite Duras

WHAT TIME IS IT WHEN THE CHICKADEE CHICKS?

—Chonda Pierce

*J*t was a dark and stormy night. Okay, it really wasn't stormy. In fact, the night was rather peaceful. The children were sound asleep, and the cat and the dog were curled up on the pillow in the garage. My husband, David, turned over on his side and told me goodnight. I lay on my back, ankles crossed, covers pulled up beneath my chin. Sigh.

I was passing over into dreamland, when I saw the flashing red clock on the nightstand by the bed. I opened my eyes wide. Big, red numbers were flashing *twelve–twelve–twelve*. Then I remembered the power had blinked off earlier in the day, which meant that every clock in the house had been knocked out. What time was it? I wondered.

I know, I thought, the Weather Channel always has the local time. So I flipped on the TV, but the only thing showing were maps of the country with big swirls, and Hs and Ls pasted all over the Midwest. My wristwatch was around somewhere, I thought, but it could be in about eight different places, and I didn't want to start tearing the place apart.

Then I did what I always do when I need an answer—just any answer. I called Mom.

"Hello, Mom," I whispered. "I was trying to set my clock, but I don't know what time it is. Do you know?"

"Oh, honey, are you having trouble sleeping again?"

"No, I'm fine. I just need to know the exact time."

"I'm not sure, honey."

"Well, look at your clock," I said.

"This one doesn't glow in the dark," she said. "I thought it did when I bought it. That's the only reason I did buy it. I may take it back to Wal-Mart tomorrow. I sure need one that glows in the dark for times just like this. I'll exchange it tomorrow."

"When did you buy it?"

"Oh, two years ago, but I've been wanting to take it back for a long time."

"Sorry your clock doesn't glow in the dark, Mom. But can you just turn on the light and tell me what time it is?"

"Oh, darling, Sammy's sleeping so soundly. If I turn on the light, I know he'll wake up. Can't I just call you in the morning, after the sun comes up, and tell you?"

I didn't want to disturb my stepfather, but I sure did want to know what time it was. "Well, what about that bird clock I bought you for your birthday? What does it say?"

"It's in the kitchen, and besides, it doesn't work at night."

"What do you mean it doesn't work at night?"

"I mean, it doesn't chirp at night," she explained. "That's so you can sleep without the bird sounds waking you up. But the last bird I heard was an oriole."

"And what time is it when the oriole chirps?"

"Eight o'clock."

"Mom, that was a long time ago."

"I know. We went to bed early."

"Maybe you can go in the kitchen and see what it says."

"The clock?"

"The clock."

"Well ..."

"What is it, Mom?"

"You see, I love the cardinal's song."

"Yes."

"And the cardinal sings at nine o'clock."

"Yes."

"Well, I never seem to be home at nine in the morning because that's when I get my hair fixed on Tuesdays; I have Bible study at that time on Wednesdays; I like to shop then on Thursdays; and on Fridays I like to come over to your place and drink coffee."

"So?"

"So by nine at night, we're usually in bed, and the clock stops chirping. That means I never hear the cardinal. That's why I set my clock up four hours. Or was it back four hours? I'm not sure. Anyway, now I can hear the cardinal."

"So I'll just add four hours or subtract. I'll figure it out."

"I may have messed up the minutes too. As a matter of fact, I'm not even sure I moved it four hours. I just kept turning it until the cardinal sang. I love to hear the cardinal sing—"

"Goodnight, Mom."

"Goodnight, darling."

I had just hung up, when the phone rang. "How would you like to have one of those clocks for Christmas?" Mom asked.

So Mom was making a dent in her Christmas list (in February), but I still didn't know what time it was. Now the Weather Channel was showing snowplows pushing through four-foot drifts and cars sliding on icy streets into the backs of other cars. Where was that little time code they always ran at the bottom of the screen?

I looked in three of the places I thought my watch could be, but it wasn't in any of them. So I sat on the edge of the bed in the dark and listened to David breathing deeply (not snoring, but close). It was so dark, so lonely, so empty, so ... timeless. So this is what the middle of the night feels like, I thought.

I couldn't stand it. I grabbed the telephone and punched in seven numbers—just random numbers. The phone rang four times when someone snatched it up on the other end and growled out a rough, "Yeah?"

"Yes, I'm sorry to call so late—and I know it is so very late—but I'm taking a survey and—"

"Lady, do you have any idea what time it is?" he growled.

"No, sir, I don't." I was as matter-of-fact as I could be.

"Well ... it's ... it's ... it's the middle of the night!" Then he hung up on me. Just like that. He was no help at all.

My phone rang immediately, and I picked it up before it could wake David. "Yes?"

Mother whispered, "Honey, I just went into the kitchen to fix myself some water, turned on the lights, and the mockingbird sang me the prettiest song. I'm telling you, you're going to love this for a Christmas present. And, by the way, it's 12:23."

"The mockingbird sings at 12:23?" I asked.

"Oh, no. It sings at 7:00. But the clock on my stove says 12:23."

"Thank you, Mother. I appreciate that."

"You're welcome. If you want, I can call you in an hour and let you hear the yellow-breasted, tufted titmouse," she added.

"That's okay. Maybe the next time around."

I went through the house and set all the clocks: the microwave, the oven, the telephone, the fax machine, and finally the clock by the bed. It was 1:00 A.M. before I crawled under the covers. David officially was snoring now, so I turned on the fan and that helped some.

It seemed like I had been asleep forever when my phone rang again. I answered it. (David just grunted.) "Hello?" I said.

"Honey," Mom said, "I know you said you didn't want to hear the tufted titmouse, but I don't think you really want to miss this." Then I heard lots of whistling and singing, like something you would hear on one of those New Age nature tapes. I could picture Mom in the kitchen, probably standing on a dining room chair and holding the phone up to her bird clock.

"Mom, do you have any idea what time it is?" I asked, once the singing stopped and I listened to what sounded like her climbing down from her chair. Just for effect, I made my voice as gruff as I could.

"Sure I do," she answered. "It's 12:23."

"Twelve twenty-three?"

"That's what my oven says."

Then I realized that's what her oven always says. But I wasn't going to let this beat me. And I wasn't going to be ugly like that mean man who had hung up on me. "Mom?" I said.

"Yes, honey?"

"What time is it on your microwave?"

"Well, let's see . . . it says 7:34."

"And the clock on the VCR?"

"Umm . . . it says 6:08."

I paused for a while before finally caving in. "Mother, does your bird clock have a chickadee song, by any chance?"

MRS. MALAPROP

—Ann Spangler

My mother has never favored her real name: Dorothy. She'd rather be called by her nicknames, Dee Dee or Dixie or just about anything but the dreaded Dorothy. But a more fitting name for Mom might be Mrs. Malaprop because every so often she comes up with a real zinger, a malapropism that puts a whole new twist on things.

Once mother was reading an article that really got her dander up. It seems the writer was advocating a rather liberal solution to the soaring problem of teenage pregnancies. Throwing up her hands, she exclaimed: "I don't know what's wrong with people today. They think they can just say: 'Give 'em all condos, give 'em all condos' and that'll fix everything."

I had to admit she had a point. Giving kids condos would put a definite pinch on the public purse and might even increase the rate of teen pregnancies. Besides, how could you possibly fit all those condos into a vending machine?

HAIR TODAY . . .
GONE TOMORROW

−Sheila Walsh

*J*f God counts every hair that falls from our heads, he must be exhausted counting mine with all the abuse I ladle out to my head of hair. I think some women have an extra gene called the "hair coloring gene." We poor souls honestly believe we can buy a little box of color in a drugstore, and we will look like the woman pictured on the box. Never happens!

But that doesn't stop me. Oh, no! I march on down the road of hair destruction in search of that elusive perfect shade.

My first foray into this bleak and unforgiving world was with a shade called "warm coffee brown." *Sounds lovely,* I thought. *I like coffee . . . this will be good.*

It turned out black. Boot-polish black. Elvira black. A-crow-died-on-your-head black. *Never mind,* I consoled myself. *I'll try again.*

And so I did with "golden ash."

How emotionally evocative, I mused. *I'll be like a tree in the fall, all shades of gold and amber.*

Well, I was half right. I did look like a tree . . . in the middle of June. It was green, green, green.

I pressed on. Next I ordered what was described as "luxurious hair" by a woman on television with big hair. I thought, *I can't go*

wrong with this. I just attach these hairpieces under my own hair for full,
flowing, glorious locks.

When I opened the box the contents looked like a row of dead
hamsters. I tried them on and had to admit I resembled a rather
sad-looking cocker spaniel.

But the greatest damage I've ever done to my hair happened
when I was eighteen years old and just about to leave my little Scot-
tish town for university in the big city of London. I was very excited
and wanted to look hip. I had long, silky hair, which I decided was
too old-fashioned. I needed a new look. So I bought a *Vogue* magazine and studied all the pictures. One model had hair that was cut in
layers and softly permed. She looked beautiful.

"Do you like this hairstyle, Mom?" I asked one evening after
dinner.

"It looks lovely, Sheila," she replied. "Why?"

"I'm thinking of having this done before I go to London."

She begged me not to. She begged me to wait and have it done
in a London salon. But I wanted to arrive as the new me. I took
the magazine picture to a small salon in my hometown of Ayr and
asked one of the stylists if she could do it.

"Oh, sure, lassie. It'll be lovely!"

I decided not to look until she was finished. I wanted a big surprise. I got one. At first I thought something was wrong with the
mirror, but then I realized I was looking at my head. I can't ade-
quately depict the fright that was me. My hair was layered different lengths on each side. It was also fried. I looked as if I'd stuck
my wet finger in an electric socket. I numbly paid and began to
walk down the road.

I talked to myself as I went. "It's not as bad as you think. It'll
be better when it's washed. Christ may return today."

Just at that moment I spotted my mom and my brother, who
were waiting for me outside a coffee shop. Stephen was laughing
so hard he was clinging to a pole to try to hold himself up. My poor
mother was attempting to make him stand up and behave, but her
efforts just caused him to laugh harder. He ended up lying on the
sidewalk.

I was eighteen then. I'm forty-two now, and thankfully I've
learned how to handle my hair. One other thing I've learned is that

my worth to God has nothing to do with how I look or feel. He is committed to me on my good hair days and on my bad hair days. And when I make a fright of my spiritual life—even committing errors that seem "permanent"—Jesus can wash them away. He is eager to do so and will never laugh, regardless of how ridiculous I look.

If today, as you look in the mirror, you wonder if this is a face only a mother could love, remember, it's a face a *Father* loves!

FIND IT AT YOUR LOCAL BOOKSTORE

—Chonda Pierce

*I*t was an exciting month. I had finally completed my first full-length comedy video and for weeks had been awaiting the news of its release. Earlier, David and I had negotiated a recording lease and distribution agreement with a music company. During the negotiations I had tried to be so professional, but deep down inside I was jumping up and down like a little girl. Soon my videos, compact discs, and cassettes would be in hundreds of Christian bookstores across the country! For years I've had this secret fantasy to be hanging out in a bookstore—perhaps looking for the latest Max Lucado book—when I'm approached by a stranger who studies first my face and then the cover of my latest video and says, "Hey—isn't this you?"

Finally the release date came. I knew they were out there. It was time to check them out. (Besides, the next Max Lucado book was out too. No harm in jetting down to the local bookstore.) I quickly discovered that I didn't make the front window, nor the rack by the cash register. I didn't even make the bargain bin! Exasperated, I finally asked the sales clerk, "Where am I?" She promptly led me to a section filled with books about psychology and left me alone.

A few days later I tried again, then again and again. Nothing. (Although I did catch up on all the Max Lucado books I was missing.) Finally, while I had several days to be home, I called my local bookstore and asked if they could check their computer to see if the project really existed. The young clerk said, "Yes, ma'am. And every time we get a few of them in, we sell them all out the same day. We have some now, but you'd better hurry. They're going quick." I couldn't believe it. Complete strangers were going into their local Christian bookstore to purchase a comedy tape of me—and not Mark Lowry!

I was so excited. My mother is going to be so proud of me, I thought. I decided to hop into my car and pick her up and take her to the bookstore and surprise her; maybe we'd even spot someone making a buy. When I got to Mom's, she was putting on her coat and scarf and was in a hurry to leave. "Oh, hi, Honey!" she greeted me. "I was just going to the mall. Want to go?" On her dining room table were about fourteen Chonda Pierce videos. I asked her where she had gotten them and what she was doing with them. She said, "Honey, I've been going to the bookstore every few days and buying these for Christmas presents. The nice young man from the bookstore just called and said some more have just come in. Your Uncle Gerald will love one of these! And Cousin Brad and Nancy—come on. We have to hurry!" She ushered me out the door.

"Going fast," the man had said. "I'll sure be glad when they put them in the bargain bin, won't you?" On the way to the mall she asked me what I was doing with all those Max Lucado books in the backseat.

"Christmas presents," I mumbled.

TOLERANCE

—Cathy Lechner

I live in a household of snorers. My husband snores, my children snore, and even my poodle snores. As I lay in bed at night, it's surround-sound snoring. I put a pillow over my head and headphones over my ears and listen to praise tapes on my Walkman. Still, stereo snoring. It is maddening. Grabbing a blanket and pillow, I have made a pilgrimage to the sofa, only to have my poodle follow me, curl up at my feet—and start snoring!

Not long after my intolerance had reached its limit, I was away on a ministry trip. Settling into the hotel bed, I remember thinking, *Tonight I get to sleep the entire night through. No crying babies and no snoring.*

I awoke the next morning greatly refreshed. Stretching lazily, I looked over at my mother, who had accompanied me.

Smiling sweetly I said, "Praise God for a good night's rest! I slept so well."

For a moment she just lay in her bed, staring at me. Then her lips tightened in a quick reply: "Well, I didn't. You snore."

Imagine my surprise! Until that moment, I had always thought Mother the very model of tolerance.

Chapter Eleven
What's Life Without a Few Wrinkles? Mighty Short!

One should never trust a woman who tells one her real age. A woman who would tell one that, would tell one anything.

—Oscar Wilde

The hardest years in life are those between ten and seventy.

—Helen Hayes

Humor purges the blood, making the body young, lively, and fit for any manner of employment.

—Robert Burton

MIDLIFE
BLISS

−Becky Freeman

*S*ometimes I look at myself in the mirror and think, *Not bad for a thirty-nine-year-old chick.* Other times I look in the mirror and wonder, *Who let that ol' goose in the henhouse?* Being smack in the middle of midlife reminds me a lot of my middle school years, when I was too old to be a cute little kid and too young to be a key-carrying, freewheeling teenager. I lived in kid purgatory for a few years there. Now I'm in middle-aged no-man's-land: too old to be considered a young chick, too young to be a wise old hen.

You know who I envy these days? Surprisingly, it is not the Cindy Crawford−types posing on covers of magazines. No, the women I envy look more like Barbara Bush. I'm looking forward to the old-hen stage−when my age will fall closer to the national speed limit. Here in the middle ages, it is becoming such an effort to keep up appearances. My makeup bag bulges with under-eye concealer, feather-proof lip liner, and a multitude of wrinkle erasers. My new skin lotion sounds like a name for a sorority house: Alpha Beta Hydroxy Complex. (With microbeads no less. I don't know what they do, but they sound impressive, don't they?) I can't wait to be far enough away from youth that I can legitimately throw in the anti-aging towel and get on with growing good and old.

How well I identify with these lines from Judith Viorst's book, *Necessary Losses.*

I'm working all day and I'm working all night
To be good-looking, healthy, and wise.
And adored.
And contented.
And brave.
And well-read.
And a marvelous hostess.
Fantastic in bed.
And bilingual.
Athletic.
Artistic.
Won't someone please stop me?

Who decided we had to try so hard to stay young? I love those happy clusters of silver-haired women you see exiting from tour buses. The kind whose very attire and demeanor says, "Who cares? I'm over seventy, and I'm entitled." The sort who have memorized the poem "When I Am Old I Shall Wear Purple" and embraced its philosophy into their lives and wardrobes. When an eighty-year-old woman wears orange stretch pants, a purple polyester shirt, Nike tennis shoes, and a hot-pink visor, folks call her "fun-loving" and "young-at-heart." But we of the pushing-forty crowd would be labeled something altogether different if we donned the same "fun-loving" ensemble. I say that it's reverse age discrimination!

The over-seventy age group also gets lots of financial perks—like Medicaid and a cheap cup of coffee at McDonalds. On the other end of the spectrum, the under-seven age group also fares well in the penny-pinching department: little kids are always being given free stuff—balloons and candy and toys in their kiddy meals. But markdowns or freebies for "in-betweeners" are nonexistent. When was the last time you saw a sign that read "Middle Age Discount"?

I've been thinking about this disparity for a while, and as a result, I have a dream, a new vision for change. Remember that Million Man March on America's capitol a few years back? Well, I think we ought to organize a Middle-Aged Women's "Waddle on

Washington" in a collective effort to make our society more midlifer friendly. I've even written a speech outlining the changes I'd like to see.

If I, a woman of the middle ages, were in charge of the country—

Donuts would be declared a health food.

Walking into a room and forgetting why you are there would be a sign of genius.

Men's pajamas, sized extra large, would be considered elegant evening wear.

Glasses and car keys would holler, "Right here!" when you ask aloud, "Where did I put them?"

The word "plump" would be interchangeable with the word "sexy" and "attractive."

Everyone would agree to always be late to everything. (This way, you see, we'd all get there at the same time. I don't know why people in charge don't consult me on these things.)

And, if I were in charge of the country—

There'd be a generic name—like maybe, "Harry"—that could be substituted anytime you forget the actual name of the dear, life-long friend you are talking to.

If I were in charge of the country—

Wrinkles on faces could be starched and ironed.

Twenty year olds could take your aerobics classes for you.

Teenagers would always be asking, "What else can I do to help you, Mother?"

If I were in charge of the country—

On long car trips, husbands would be required to periodically ask their wives, "How would you like to stop at that cute little gift shop, have some tea and scones, and shop for an hour or so?"

A sense of humor and a kindhearted nature would be valued more highly than being skinny or young or beautiful.

The End

If we could somehow manage to get these few items changed, then the word *midlife* might not be paired so often with the words like *crisis* or *crazies* or *malaise*. Instead, we'd hear maturing women announce, "I'm in Midlife Bliss," or "I'm at that ol' Midlife Prime— I love my life, and I like who I am. God is good."

Come to think of it—I *am* in love with my life. I *do* like who I am. And God is good. Even at thirty-nine and holding.

Maybe we ought to hold off on that Waddle to Washington for a while. For even though our midlife bodies are a little baggier here and there, these mid decades can actually be the most fulfilling of our life. I recently heard a man say, "I think women have this incredible 'blossoming thing' happen when they turn forty. They get an extra boost of confidence or something, and it's like they suddenly say, 'Look out world! I'm coming out of my shell!'"

I think he may be right. But before I hatch out of my middle-aged shell and go take over the world I have one last important question to ask:

"Does anybody remember where I put my car keys?"

KEEP YOUR TWEEZERS TO YOURSELF!

–Gracie Malone

*O*ne morning we decided to visit "Mama," my 103-year-old grandmother who lived in the nursing home. I settled in the car's back seat next to Mom as my sister Lois climbed in front with Aunt Grace. Feeling good, I closed my eyes to bask in the sunshine and listen to the older women folks chatter.

I opened my eyes when my eighty-four-year-old mother started fumbling through her purse. From the depths of her bag, she retrieved a shiny surgical-steel instrument and polished it with her hanky. I wondered what she was doing until suddenly I recognized her tweezers. Without one word of warning, my mother took aim, and plucked my chin. She proudly displayed her prize: one curly, half-inch long, silver hair. Her mission accomplished, Mom replace the tweezers in a tiny leather case and deposited it back in her purse without missing a beat in her conversation.

As I rubbed my chin, I admitted to myself that I wasn't crazy about getting old. In fact, I'm downright chicken about it. During recent years, I've ducked a midlife crisis, plunged headlong into the empty nest syndrome, and now, just as I'm winging my way toward liberty and leisure, I'm in a flap about senior citizenship.

At the nursing home, Mother slipped her arm in mine as we walked down the long corridor and into Mama's room. Standing by her bed, I felt overwhelmed by my grandmother's frail form barely visible beneath the sheets. Mama's lived entirely too long, I thought. *Why doesn't she give up? Why doesn't God take her on home?* But soon my perspective changed.

Like a hen hovering over her brood of chicks, my mother fluttered and fussed over Mama. She washed her face with a warm cloth, brushed her hair, and applied lotion to her gnarled hands. I overheard Mother clucking tenderly, "Everything's okay. I'm here. I love you, Mama." My heart melted as I thought about my rich heritage from these two women, and suddenly 103 years didn't seem enough.

The next weekend, I checked into the hospital for mini-surgery. Since I'll probably live an eon, (if genetics have anything to do with it) I decided to take care of my health. The procedure the doctor performed was, in my opinion, nothing short of a miracle. Through a tiny incision he removed all the stuff I didn't need, then using a little camera, with flash attachment, he took pictures of everything I had left.

At my next appointment, the doctor proudly displayed eight-by-ten glossies of my innards. As he pointed out my "inward parts," I felt apprehensive. He tapped one picture with his pen and said, "This is your liver." He sighed, clicked his tongue approvingly, and with deep appreciation in his voice, added, "What a fine liver!" When I'm feeling uneasy, just one little compliment can make my day–*any* kind of compliment.

As I left the doctor's office and strutted toward my car, I kept repeating in a giddy voice, "I have a *fine* liver. I have a fine *liver!*" I not only felt healthy, I felt internally gorgeous all afternoon.

I suppose most of us women are chickenhearted about one thing or another. But it doesn't take much to make us feel confident. With just one word of kindness or a simple compliment, we sprout wings and fly. So, next time we gather, let's talk about things that are friendly and nice. And remember, whatever you do, puh-leeeeeze, keep your tweezers in your purse!

LOVE
THOSE
WRINKLES!

–Liz Curtis Higgs

$\mathcal{S}$oon after my fortieth (how did they know?), I received an envelope in the mail filled with slick literature about a wrinkle-minimizing system. Not just a cream, not merely a moisturizer, this was all that and more: a *pill*. A pill "based on the work of a famed Scandinavian skin specialist" (who wasn't putting his/her name on *anything*). It was advertised as a "quantum leap in the war on wrinkles ... works from the inside out!"

Well, I am working on my wrinkles from the inside out. My goal is to stay plump enough to keep those wrinkles nicely filled up and therefore save $154.85 on a three-month supply of their wrinkle-minimizing system. If you're going to spend $1.72 a day, why not just buy three jelly donuts? It would accomplish the same thing and be more fun.

My friend and favorite funny lady, Jeanne Robertson, fifty-three, has been speaking and traveling the country for thirty years. As Jeanne puts it, "At this point, I lie in the bed at night and hear myself wrinkling. It wakes me up. The wrinkling comes in loud and clear because it is happening so near my ears. One night my husband sat right up in the bed and whispered, 'The house is settling ... or is that you wrinkling again?'" Children are fascinated by wrinkles. Beverly, fifty-eight, from Colorado admits, "My little granddaughter, age four, wonders why I have so many cracks in my face."

Our son, Matthew, tries to count the rings in my neck to determine my age, like an ancient sequoia. Daughter Lillian likes to fit her little finger in the grooves so she can, in her words, "drive all over my face." Lovely.

Speaking of driving, let's climb into the car with Virginia, fifty-four, from Oklahoma:

Our family was traveling down the highway for a weekend outing and I was working on a stitchery project in the front seat. As I was busily stitching, I got this feeling that someone was staring at me and looked up to find my daughter, Betty, nine, leaning over the backseat carefully examining my face. With all the innocence in the world she sweetly proclaimed, "Mommy, did you know that your Oil of Olay isn't working?!"

Or as Maxine, forty-seven, says, "Oil of Delay is my best friend!"

I long for the days when I could face the world *sans* makeup, when moisturizer was something you smoothed on your legs after a day in the sun, when Noxzema and water kept you looking dewy fresh around the clock, when your face didn't look as though you slept in it. But the good news is ... wrinkles not only come from time and the sun, they also come from laughing at the absurdities of life, which increase exponentially after forty. They also come from looking surprised when your child hands you a woolly worm from the garden. They come from smiling when you see an old friend who is as wrinkled as you are. They are a roadmap of experiences that you alone have enjoyed.

I'm learning to embrace the psalmist's words, "The lines have fallen to me in pleasant places." Even if they have fallen on my face, at least I can keep track of them there, knowing every single wrinkle was earned with time well spent.

PRAYER IN OLD AGE

—Attributed to a Seventeeth-Century Nun

Lord, you know better than I know myself that I am getting older and will someday be old. Keep me from the fatal habit of thinking I must say something on every subject and on every occasion. Release me from craving to straighten out everybody's affairs. Make me thoughtful but not moody, helpful but not bossy. With my vast store of wisdom it seems a pity not to use it all, but you know, Lord, that I want a few friends at the end. Keep my mind from the recital of endless details—give me wings to come to the point. Seal my lips on my aches and pains. They are increasing, and my love of rehearsing them is becoming sweeter. I dare not ask for grace enough to enjoy the tales of others' pains, but help me to endure them with patience. I dare not ask for improved memory, but for a growing humility and a lessening cocksureness when my memory seems to clash with the memories of others. Teach me the glorious lesson that occasionally I may be mistaken. Keep me reasonably sweet. I do not want to be a saint—some of them are so hard to live with—but a sour old woman is one of the crowning works of the devil. Give me the ability to see good things in unexpected places, and talents in unexpected people. And give me the grace to tell them so.

Chapter Twelve
We Need a Little Christmas Cheer

There are some people who want to throw their arms 'round you simply because it is Christmas; there are other people who want to strangle you simply because it is Christmas.

—Robert Lynd

A lovely thing about Christmas is that it's compulsory, like a thunderstorm, and we all go through it together.

—Garrison Keillor

HO,
HO,
NO!

−Nancy Kennedy

It was a dark and stormy December afternoon, and our Christmas tree sat in the living room undecorated. My husband and I had argued the night before over the spiritual significance of tinsel (I said there isn't any; he insisted a fourth wise man might have brought some).

So there we sat with an undecorated tree in the house and the Minnesota Vikings and Dallas Cowboys on TV. With Barry absorbed in the game, I started reading the holiday issue of a women's magazine and got an idea so great I knew it would cement our relationship. We were going to make a gingerbread house.

I could hardly wait to bring Barry the tidings of great joy. But his face clearly said, "I'll give you hard cash if you'll just go away," as Dallas led the Vikings into the second half.

"Come on, I've got everything ready in the kitchen." Barry mumbled something that sounded like "Aarrghh, rucashdretsh, errrgff," but he did follow me to the kitchen.

I've seen enough Ozzie and Harriet reruns to know that couples thrive on this kind of stuff. The happy husband and smiling wife approach the task together—chuckling as a little flour gets tossed around the room—and then forge ahead with just the right amount of playful banter. This was going to be great!

We began with balls of sticky, gray dough. Technically, gingerbread isn't supposed to be gray, but we were out of ginger, cinnamon, and molasses. I improvised with white corn syrup, and Barry slathered the dough with shortening, convinced that it would roll out better that way.

With gray slime up to our elbows, our joint project became a little less playful. Barry ended up back in the living room, watching the end of the game while I rolled the dough, cut out the pieces, and put them in the oven.

About the time the smoke alarm went off (the excess shortening caught fire when it dripped onto the heating element), Dallas won the game. Barry wandered back into the kitchen to apologize, open the windows, and fan out the smoke.

Then he stared at the lopsided, burnt gingerbread structure, while I set out bowls of candy corn, jelly beans, and M&Ms. "We could scrape the burnt stuff off," he said hopefully. "Maybe with enough candy it won't look too terrible."

The next two hours we scraped, assembled, and trimmed. One of us would hold up a wall while the other slopped frosting between the seams. We invented an ingenious means of repairing cracks and designed elaborate braces to hold the walls in place. I realized that we worked well together after all. Then, just as I opened my mouth to declare our house (and our marriage) a success, I discovered that all the red M&Ms were gone. I couldn't make poinsettias without them.

"The picture in the magazine shows poinsettias by the front door," I pointed out, "but you ate all the red M&Ms!"

"I didn't eat them all," Barry retorted. "We used most of them already."

Then he picked a red M&M off the windowsill of our crooked little house and popped it into his mouth.

Our gazes locked, I ripped a spice drop off his snow flower and chewed it. Loudly.

We continued prying and chewing and swallowing pieces of candy until finally, in a moment of temporary psychopathic imbalance, one of us broke off a piece of the roof and ate it.

"I can't believe you did that," I cried, slamming my fist down on the table. The rest of the roof caved in.

"I can't believe *you* did *that*."

We looked at each other sheepishly over the crumbled ginger-bread house. Feeling silly for arguing and slightly queasy from eating so much candy, we gathered up the remains.

As we trudged out to the garbage can, the moon lit up the night. We drew close to each other, looked toward the east and saw a single star. Suddenly, I didn't care about the gingerbread house.

"Barry," I said, "how does this sound? Next December we could make a life-size plaster of Paris nativity set for the front lawn."

At first I thought he said, "Sure, no problem." But it might have just been "aarrghh, rucashdretsh, errrgff!"

PICTURE PERFECT

—Marti Attoun

*E*very Christmas, we get at least one photo card of a festive family smiling around a dust-free piano or fireplace. And every year I promise myself that my family will star in one of these cards the next year.

We finally attempted one of these photo greetings. Not having a piano to lean upon and lend us culture was the least of our problems.

"You want me to shoot a what?" my husband asked, dumbfounded.

"I want you to put that camera on a tripod and take one decent family picture for a Christmas card. The grannies will love it," I told him. "Now, we need to act quickly while the baby's in a good mood. Let's all hurry and get cleaned up."

I clapped my hands and tried to rustle up some holiday harmony. The baby clapped his hands back and showed off his sharp little biters. The two older kids growled.

"You've already got seventeen school pictures of me," my ten-year-old son pointed out. "How many pictures do you need, anyway?"

I reminded him that hair was looping his nose in all seventeen of those poses. I also introduced a new concept to him: the idea

209

that some loving families (like our own) have their pictures taken *together*, instead of solo.

"Sure, Mom. Just like you tried to tell us that other families eat dinner together. Get real."

My eight-year-old daughter was enthusiastic too.

"I'll get in the stupid picture, but I'm not going to change clothes," she announced. I checked her over from head to toe. She had been playing with her swirl-and-twirl-a-paint. Her sweatshirt had been the canvas.

"Okay. Just stand in the back so we can't see your spots, and go brush your hair."

"Only my bangs," she said.

"Of course, silly."

I went back to work on my son's basic good nature (the son I remember before he teleported to the twelfth realm of the fifth world on some Nintendo game).

"Humor your mother, dear," I said. "I'd like to have one pretty color picture of all of us to give to the grannies for Christmas. If we start now and the picture's ugly, we'll have time for a reshoot." I could see that I wasn't getting through to his good nature, so I whispered the magic words I knew he could understand, "Smile and there'll be two bucks in it for you."

He thought for a moment.

"Do I have to put my shoes on?" he asked.

"Of course not. You can sit on your feet."

Before any more objections could be raised, I turned the gas up on the fireplace log and raked the mantel clean of car keys, dirty glasses, and a broken aquarium pump. As soon as it looked picture-perfect, I summoned the photographer.

"Sorry. The battery's dead in the flash," he said. "We'll have to shoot it outdoors or forget it."

"I have a great idea," said our daughter, her bangs now lacquered into an ocean wave. "Let's take the picture in the tree-house." She had such a pretty say-cheese smile that I hated to refuse.

We clambered into the treehouse, and the photographer secured the tripod on a sturdy limb. The paid model sat on his cold, dirty feet in one lawnchair. His sister crouched behind so her splotches wouldn't show. I sat in the other lawnchair and held the baby. The photographer cleared a spot so he could dash into the picture.

He set the timer and it started to buzz.

"Say *'Merry Christmas From Our House,'* everybody!" I hollered.

The baby grunted, turned red, and began to kick his heels. The paid model started scratching his armpits and making ape noises to entertain the baby. His sister shouted a countdown loud enough to activate the Neighborhood Watch program. The photographer leaned so far into the picture that he obscured my smile.

But you should have seen the smile wreathing the neighbor's face as he stood in front of his evergreen in his red flannel shirt watching our family charade.

I quickly snatched the camera and snapped the guy's picture. He looked just like a Christmas card.

I think the grannies are going to love him on the family greeting card this year.

THIS LITTLE PIGGY WENT TO DAY CARE

–Connie Breedlove

*O*ne year my sister, Malvina, and I merged our energies and opened a day care business at her house. It was very successful—we had several kids, and we really worked to make it go.

We had craft classes for them, hot lunches, and kindergarten pick-up and delivery. All in all, it was a working mom's dream, if I say so myself. It was also our dream, because having a successful, home-based business was something we had both always wanted.

But the dream soon took on nightmare characteristics, and not just your run-of-the-mill type nightmares. I'm talking Freddy Krueger here.

It started with our decision to sell homemade candy. Now, I'll be the first to admit that the candy business probably wouldn't have caused a problem by itself; the pig was the big problem—even though it was a small pig. But I'm getting ahead of myself.

It was Christmas time, and we had this great family recipe for a date-nut candy log that we decided to try to sell for extra Christmas money.

In the afternoons, when the kids were having their naps, my sister would take candy samples to give out in the stores and get orders for the candy. I would stay with the kids and make candy to fill the orders we already had. It was working out great.

212

Then one afternoon Malvina was out getting orders, the kids were napping, and I was up to my ears in date-nut candy when the phone rang. When I answered it, my husband's voice said, in an overly cheerful tone, "Hi! What are you doing?"

I couldn't understand why he was asking me that; he knew what I was doing.

"Well," I said, flicking a crumb of candy off my shoulder, "for the last hour I've been soaking in a warm bubble bath, and now I'm sitting here waiting for the maid to finish fixing my lunch."

He laughed and made small talk for a few minutes until finally, he said, "Well, I've got to get back to work. Oh, by the way, I got a pig today."

"By the way, you got a pig today?" I repeated.

"Yeah, I was going to surprise you, but I couldn't wait. So, what do you think?"

"Flowers would have been nice," I said.

"Honey, this was such a good deal, I couldn't pass it up," he said.

"But it's Christmas time, how can we afford a pig?"

"That's the best part! It was free!"

"Free?" I said, almost afraid to ask the rest of the question. "Why would anyone give away a pig? And even if it was free, we don't have a pig house or a fence or anything."

"It's not called a pig house, it's called a pigsty," he said, his voice dripping with patience.

"Why was it free and where are we keeping it?" I said, my voice totally devoid of patience.

"Let me explain before you get upset. This is a very small pig—"

"So, where are we going to keep a very small pig?" I asked.

There was a long enough pause to cause my apprehension level to hit TILT.

"We'll have to keep it in the house for a while," he finally managed to say.

Now, keep in mind, this happened several years before people started keeping miniature pigs as pets. This happened when a pig was a pig and by any other name was still a pig.

"No!"

"Honey, it's so tiny! It's in a shoe box!"

"No, no, no, *NO*."

"Its mother rejected it," he said.

"I don't blame her," I answered.

"We'll talk about it this evening. I've got to get back to work. Bye," he said, and I was left listening to the dial tone.

The first thing Len did when we got home that night was to take the pig out of the box and give it to me to hold. This man was a real pro. He knew exactly what he was doing. That pig really was so tiny that it was in a shoebox, and it was really cute. There I was, holding that sweet, little pig while I told Len how impossible it would be to take care of one so small.

He reached over and took the pig from me, saying, "You're right. I don't know what I was thinking. This pig would require way too much care, and neither one of us has that much time."

"What are you going to do with it?" I asked, hoping he would say he knew of a home for pigs.

"It'll have to be destroyed," he said, putting on his jacket.

"No!" I yelled, snatching the pig from him with all the ferocity of an enraged mama pig who was protecting her own.

"But, honey, there's no way you'll have time to do this."

"Yes, I will, I will."

"Okay, if you're sure," he said, taking an eyedropper out of his coat pocket. "You can feed it with this. I'll set the alarm to go off every two hours so it won't miss a feeding. Goodnight, little mama."

As I watched him disappear down the hall and into our bedroom, my motherly instincts suddenly began to wane. He will never know how close he came to getting hit in the back of the head with a flying pig.

The next morning, I got up with circles under my eyes from three nighttime feedings. I felt guilty because the last time I fed the pig, I found myself mentally measuring it for a hoagie bun.

After I had a couple of cups of coffee to get my nerve geared up, I called my sister to try and explain why I was going to have to bring a pig with me that morning.

"I think this is going to be one of those days," she said, laughing. "I thought you just said you were bringing a pig with you."

"I did say that," I said.

"What do you mean, 'a pig'?" she asked, still not realizing I meant a PIG.

"It's a baby pig, and I have to bring it with me because it has to be fed every two hours."

"No!"

"It's a very small pig," I said.

"No! No! No!"

"Its mother rejected it."

Talk about role reversal! I was playing Len, my sister was playing me, and the pig was playing an innocent bystander.

"Look," she said, "even if it is a small pig we can't keep it here because if the parents find out we're keeping a pig in the house, they'll take their kids out of day care. And when word gets around, our candy sales are history."

I hadn't thought of that.

"I just don't know what to do about it," I said.

She thought for a minute and then she said, "Okay, bring it with you, and when you get here, honk the horn. I'll get the kids busy in the other end of the house while you sneak the pig down into the basement."

That plan came off without a hitch. It worked perfectly! It was such a success that after the pig was safely hidden in the basement, I had a tremendous feeling of exhilaration, as if we had just pulled off the hoax of the century. You'd have thought we were dealing with the CIA instead of a group of five year olds.

Well, we set the timer on the oven to go off every two hours, and when it buzzed, Malvina would get the kids' attention so I could run down to the basement and feed the pig. This was pretty exhausting, but it worked.

But by that afternoon, my sister was beginning to run out of things with which to distract the kids, and they were beginning to look at her as if maybe she was ready for the Big Day Care Center in the sky.

In between feedings, we were catching up on our candy orders. The recipe was incredibly hard to mix since it had chopped dates, marshmallows, pecans, and graham cracker crumbs—it was like trying to mix cold tar.

That afternoon we managed to mix, roll, and wrap thirty-two of those candy logs. We felt as if we had been pulled through a knothole backward, but we also had a tremendous feeling of accomplishment.

Until . . .

While we were standing there admiring our thirty-two date nut rolls stacked like cordwood on the cabinet, I discovered a button missing from my cuff—a button that hadn't been missing when I started mixing the candy.

We searched every nook and cranny in the house, from kitchen to basement. That was the most intense game of "button, button, who's got the button?" that either one of us had ever played.

But it was to no avail. Finally, we both stood mutely staring at the only place we hadn't searched, the thirty-two candy rolls, stacked like cordwood on the cabinet.

"Do you think it's in one of those?" my sister asked in a very tired, lackluster voice.

"Maybe," I said with about one degree less enthusiasm than she was registering.

There was a long silence.

"So, what now?" I asked. She just stood there shaking her head for the longest time. I was beginning to think she had developed some sort of nervous tic. Maybe the weight of that missing button was the proverbial "straw that broke the camel's back."

Then she began laughing, quietly at first, like it was some private joke only she knew about. Then the laughter got louder and louder, and the tears began to run down her face and she was gasping for breath.

"What?" I asked, laughing just because she was.

But she couldn't answer. She wasn't even making a sound now. Her mouth was open, and she was obviously laughing, but with a temporary loss of sound.

The harder she laughed, the harder I laughed, until we were both sitting on the floor, almost helpless with laughter.

Finally she said, as she tried desperately to catch her breath, "I know what to do about the candy."

I was laughing too hard to even ask what she had in mind.

But that was all right, she didn't need a straight line, she was on a roll.

"When we deliver the candy, we'll tell them that we hid a button in one of the candy rolls and the person who gets the candy with the button wins a pig!"

That was too much. Everything became a blur of pigs, buttons, candy, and kids, and we laughed and laughed and laughed. After that, we felt sooooo much better!

We decided to go ahead and take a chance on delivering the candy, and that was good because a couple of days later we found the button in the silverware drawer.

Unfortunately, the little pig was too young and it didn't make it, but if it had survived, I don't know what we would have done with it. It would definitely have been a pet. We'd have ended up sharing our television and snacks every evening with a three-hundred-pound couch potato.

God is such a good God, and he has put us together in a wonderful and awesome way. When our nose tickles, he has given us the ability to sneeze. When we're tired, he has given us the pleasure of a good, deep yawn. And when things go wrong, he has given us the ability to sit back and laugh at ourselves—and that is definitely wonderful and awesome!

I LOVE CATS!

−Elisa Morgan

$\mathcal{B}$efore I tell you this story, I need to assure you that I love cats. I always have. When I was eight, I begged my mother, who was a dog lover, for a cat. She ignored my pleas, stalled my overtures, and then finally gave in. In the years that followed, I have self-sacrificially cared for my cats as I would have cared for my own children. I rescued one from the top of a forty-foot poplar tree. I gave shots to another who was diagnosed with a fatal disease, and I actually nursed her back to health. In the middle of the night, I've endured kneading paws in the nape of my neck. While immersed in a novel, I've made room on my lap to accommodate an incessant need for cuddling. I've willingly succumbed to my own children when they've pleaded for a cat−one each−and have taken it upon myself to litter-box train and care for these new additions to our family in the years when my children were too young to care for them independently. And though sometimes I've been miffed, I've obediently cleaned up fur balls and other messes left behind by my cats. So as you read the following, remember this: I really do love cats.

One winter morning, I was shoveling snow off the driveway, minding my own business. My neighbor pulled her car up to the curb, rolled down her window, and presented her Christmas-gift-of-the-year idea to me. "How about," she suggested, "if we help our daughters make matching sweatshirts for each other to exchange at the neighborhood children's party? We won't tell them that they too are receiving one, only that they're making one. They'll be so surprised when they tear open their gifts to find them matching!"

Quickly, heartily, enthusiastically, I agreed. Moments later, watching her car's exhaust trail up the street, I realized that I had no clue about how to make a sweatshirt myself, much less assist Eva in the process. A panic-filled phone call to my neighbor later that afternoon left me armed with a list of necessary purchases from the fabric store and detailed instructions. I was to buy a large white sweatshirt, the Daisy Kingdom bunny applique, and a specific selection of pink, blue, green, and black fabric paint.

Like most Decembers, this particular December was frantic with chores that promised to make Christmas magical but in reality only created a grumpy mom. On Saturday morning, hours before the children's Christmas party, Eva and I descended the stairs to our basement, with paraphernalia in hand and anticipation in heart. Choosing the only flat, clean surface in our basement on which to work, we carefully laid out the sweatshirt, applique, and paints atop the washer and dryer.

The sweat beaded up on my brow as my nervous fingers peeled back the applique and I pressed the iron down on the shirt. At my elbow, Eva giggled with excitement. *Ah . . . Isn't this great?* Mother-daughter bonding time. Bonding, bonding, bonding, are we bonding? I checked the applique. Yes, we were bonding.

Next came the green paint around the grass. Then the black paint. *Oh, this is a challenge.* "I'll do that, Eva," I said. Black paint on a white sweatshirt, around the edges of the Daisy Kingdom bunnies, up around the ears. *Hey! We can do this!* All done, we bounded up the stairs to attend to other tasks.

Two hours later I decided I'd better check on the sweatshirt. *Is it dry yet? It's so good to have that checked off my list today!* I trundled down the stairs and approached the washer and dryer.

Something looked askew.

I looked more closely at the washer and dryer. The sweatshirt was tilted at a bizarre angle on the lid of the washer, its long arm dangling precariously off the edge.

I was concerned.

On my tiptoes, more gingerly now, I moved forward, afraid of what I might discover. Another step. Black spots covered the lid of my white washing machine. Inky smudges trailed across the sweatshirt, over the washing machine, down its side, and over the floor where they weren't before and where they shouldn't ever be.

I bent to inspect these spots. I did not need a magnifying glass. I could tell at a glance that these were no ordinary black spots. They had the size and shape of a paw print. Measuring the circumference of the paw print, I ascertained that it was the print of the large, white cat—the one that *used to* belong to Eva.

Here's where it gets a little sticky, this story. The sweatshirt had to be wrapped by four o'clock for the neighborhood Christmas party. It was now 2:00 P.M. There was no time to re-create a replacement and get it dry and wrapped. We had to go to this party. I couldn't let my neighbor or her daughter down! What would they think? We were the ones who knew Jesus. Most of the rest of the neighborhood didn't.

But instead of problem-solving a present at the moment, I prowled around on my hands and knees in search of a white cat that used to be welcome in our house. I made my way through dust balls, stacks of boxes, and set-aside holiday decorations until I found him cowering under a party piñata.

He looked at me and I looked at him. I was bigger, but he was faster. I lunged. He sprang. I caught him. All kinds of options ran through my head. Hitting, kicking, throwing. *No, I can't do that. That would hurt him. No, no, no. No matter how much a mess he's made, I mustn't hurt this cat.*

So I bit the cat. Right on the top of his head in the furry part below his ear. I didn't bite him hard. I promise. It was just a nibble.

Remember, I really do love cats.

Staring at my cat and then at the paw-printed sweatshirt, I knew I was doomed. The black blotches across the white surfaces mirrored my own imperfections. There was no way I could complete my end of the deal with my neighbor. Her daughter would be disappointed when there was no box for her to open. No matching sweatshirt surprise. No perfect present.

I got in my car, drove to the fabric store, and bought another large white sweatshirt and Daisy Kingdom bunny applique. I wrapped them up in a box with a note that promised the finished product as soon as the paint could dry. Later, at the party, my neighbor beamed. Her daughter hugged mine while my daughter gasped with delight over the matching sweatshirt she received. I smiled with relief, still picking the fur from my teeth.

ALL I
WANT FOR
CHRISTMAS

–Charlene Ann Baumbich

For a long time I've wanted to have my picture taken with Santa as a gift to my boys, who I knew would appreciate Mom's sense of fun and adventure. (Right, boys? And if you don't, remember Santa is watching, and Santa will be miffed to learn you don't have those photos of Mom and Santa prominently displayed in your homes, thereby causing Santa to perhaps reevaluate next year's stocking loot!) But the last few years, when I've happened upon a Santa in a mall, the lines have always been too long and I've been in too big a hurry to follow through on this whim.

This year was different. I found Santa alone but for an elf (the photographer), one baby on his lap, and two parents hurling themselves around like goons trying to get their precious one to smile. Inclement weather and hazardous road conditions opened this opportunity. And so I seized the moment and told the elf I'd like to have my picture taken, using the holiday special rate of one five-by-seven and two wallet-size photos for under ten dollars. Big George could take the five-by-seven to his office. (Ditto goes to George about the loot!) The elf asked my name and told me the obvious: I would be next—as soon as the threesome either got a good picture or expired from their aerobic drama. (My words, not the elf's.)

"Santa, this is Charlene. She'd like to have her picture taken with you."

"Well, hello, Charlene. Come talk to Santa." He was kind; his face registered no shock or scorn.

"Santa, my gift to you will be that I won't sit on your lap; I'll sit on the cushion next to you."

No arguments from Santa.

The two of us cuddled up for the photo and the flash blinked, announcing completion of my mission.

"Charlene, what would you like Santa to bring you for Christmas?" Santa asked.

I hadn't thought this far ahead; the photo was all I'd wanted. (Not thinking ahead is something I'm famous for, but then, Santa probably already knew that.)

Without batting an eye or hesitating for a moment, the following—which was the total truth—erupted from my lips on this particular Friday.

"Santa, I'm having a hysterectomy next Wednesday, and I'd like swift healing." Although I couldn't believe what I'd uttered, I was not surprised, as this disbelief of my own utterings is routine.

Then Santa's blue eyes looked into mine, as though they were piercing my very soul. He said, "I'll pray for you, and so will Mrs. Claus."

I was so moved that I immediately began to cry. "Oh, Santa, you couldn't have told me anything more perfect." Realizing that I was now standing before him bawling, I added, "Perhaps more estrogen would be nice too."

Santa smiled. I thanked him one last time and walked away, but not before saying, "You know, you still come to my house in the middle of the night every year, even though my baby is twenty-five years old."

"I know," he said.

Well, the photos were swell. But they were secondary to my experience. I told nearly everyone I saw about my meeting with Santa. "It was as though Christ became incarnate in this Santa to assure me that everything would be okay," I heard myself repeating time after time. "I felt so calm." My friend, Janet, a sister in Christ whom I'd told, faxed me before surgery to let me know she was praying for me. She prayed that my surgery go as scheduled. She prayed for my recovery, for my relationships to be blessing to me and God, for the doctors to have wisdom. And "I pray," she wrote, "that Mr. and Mrs. Claus have their prayers answered." She too had been affected by my story.

As it turned out, surgery went pretty well. Two hours after surgery, however, my heart rate began to drop—all the way to zero, which, as one doctor said, "we thought was a little too low." I became a flat-liner on the monitors (which means you're on your way to dead), and nurse Jaci had to administer CPR. I snapped right back, thanks to the grace of God and Jaci's quick actions. I have recuperated just fine.

But I cannot begin to tell you how many times during and since my recovery I've revisited my encounter with Santa. I am in awe of how I felt so blessed and lifted right into the presence of Jesus when Santa talked to me. In fact, God's arms, looking very much like Santa's, can be seen wrapped around me in the photo. Of this I am sure.

NOTES

The compiler gratefully acknowledges publishers and individuals who granted permission to reprint the material in this book. In a few cases, it was not possible to trace the original authors. The compiler will be happy to rectify this if and when the authors contact her by writing to Zondervan Publishing House, 5300 Patterson Ave., S.E., Grand Rapids, MI 49503. Each piece is noted in the order it appears in the book. (Note: material that is public domain or that was written by Ann Spangler is not included in this list.)

"A Laugh a Day Puts Wrinkles in the Right Places" by Liz Curtis Higgs taken from *Only Angels Can Wing It* (Nashville, TN: Thomas Nelson Publishers, 1995). Used by permission.

"A Mouthful of Laughter" by Barbara Johnson taken from *Joy Breaks* by Patsy Clairmont, Barbara Johnson, Marilyn Meberg, Luci Swindoll. Copyright © 1997 by Women of Faith, Inc. Used by permission of Zondervan Publishing House.

"Cross My Heart" by Liz Curtis Higgs from *Forty Reasons Why Life Is More Fun after the Big 4-0* (Nashville, TN: Thomas Nelson Publishers, 1997). Used by permission.

"Techno-Wonders of the Modern Age" taken from *Duh-Votions* by Sue Buchanan. Copyright © 1999 by Sue Buchanan. Used by permission of Zondervan Publishing House.

"The Mammogram" taken from *Boomerang Joy* by Barbara Johnson. Copyright © 1998 by Barbara Johnson. Used by permission of Zondervan Publishing House.

The quoted material on pages 28-29 is reprinted from And How Are We Feeling Today? by Kathryn Hammer © 1993. Used with permission of NTC/Contemporary Publishing Group, Inc..

"The Infamous Bra" by Thelma Wells taken from *OverJoyed* by Patsy Clairmont, Barbara Johnson, Marilyn Meberg, Luci Swindoll, Sheila Walsh, and Thelma Wells. Copyright © 1999 by Women of Faith, Inc. Used by permission of Zondervan Publishing House.

"I Was a Victim of Tsk-Tsk-ers" taken from *Duh-Votions* by Sue Buchanan. Copyright © 1999 by Sue Buchanan. Used by permission of Zondervan Publishing House.

"Lookin' Good" taken from *God Uses Cracked Pots* by Patsy Clairmont, a Focus on the Family book published by Tyndale House. Copyright © 1996 by Patsy Clairmont. All rights reserved. International copyright secured. Used by permission.

"In the Pink" by Liz Curtis Higgs taken from *Only Angels Can Wing It* (Nashville, TN: Thomas Nelson Publishers, 1995). Used by permission.

"Overcoming with Worms" is taken from *A View from the Porch Swing* by Becky Freeman. Copyright © 1994, Broadman & Holman Publishers. All rights reserved. Used by permission.

"Keep on Ticking" by Bodie Thoene. This article first appeared in *Today's Christian Woman* magazine (September/October 1990), a publication of Christianity Today, Inc. Used by permission.

"Night Life" taken from *God Uses Cracked Pots* by Patsy Clairmont, a Focus on the Family book published by Tyndale House. Copyright © 1996 by Patsy Clairmont. All rights reserved. International copyright secured. Used by permission.

"Hanky Panky" taken from *Mama Said There'd Be Days Like This* by Charlene Ann Baumbich. Copyright © 1995 by Charlene Ann Baumbich. Published by Servant Publications, Box 8617, Ann Arbor, Michigan, 48107. Used with permission.

"Aphrodisiacs" by Betty Smartt Carter. This article first appeared in *Marriage Partnership* magazine (Spring 1998), a publication of Christianity Today, Inc. Used by permission.

"Part Man, Part Barca-Lounger" taken from *Duh-Votions* by Sue Buchanan. Copyright © 1999 by Sue Buchanan. Used by permission of Zondervan Publishing House.

"Finished Yet?" by Sheila Walsh taken from *OverJoyed* by Patsy Clairmont, Barbara Johnson, Marilyn Meberg, Luci Swindoll, Sheila Walsh, and Thelma Wells. Copyright © 1999 by Women of Faith, Inc. Used by permission of Zondervan Publishing House.

"'Twas the Night before New Year's" by Nancy Kennedy. This article first appeared in *Marriage Partnership* magazine (Winter 1995), a publication of Christianity Today, Inc. Used by permission.

"Sweet Spirit" by Karen M. Feaver. This article first appeared in *Marriage Partnership* magazine (Winter 1995), a publication of Christianity Today, Inc. Used by permission.

"Someone to Watch Over Me" by Janell Wheeler. This article was first published in *Christian Reader* magazine (March/April 1997), a publication of Christianity Today, Inc. Used by permission.

"Romantically Impaired" by Nancy Kennedy. This article first appeared in *Marriage Partnership* magazine (Summer 1993), a publication of Christianity Today, Inc. Used by permission.

"Miracle on Second Street" taken from *Mama Said There'd Be Days Like This.* By Charlene Ann Baumbich. Copyright © 1995 by Charlene Ann Baumbich. Published by Servant Publications, Box 8617, Ann Arbor, Michigan, 48107. Used with permission.

"What a Guy!" by Marilyn Meberg taken from *OverJoyed* by Patsy Clairmont, Barbara Johnson, Marilyn Meberg, Luci Swindoll, Sheila Walsh, and Thelma Wells. Copyright © 1999 by Women of Faith, Inc. Used by permission of Zondervan Publishing House.

"In Silliness and Health," by Liz Curtis Higgs from *Help, I'm Laughing and I Can't Get Up* (Nashville, TN: Thomas Nelson Publishers, 1998). Used by permission.

"Stop the Treadmill, I Gotta Get Off" by Charlene Ann Baumbich. This article first appeared in *Marriage Partnership* magazine (Fall 1993), a publication of Christianity Today, Inc. Used by permission.

"The Bathroom That Ate Our Budget" by Nancy Kennedy. This article was first published in *Marriage Partnership* magazine (Winter 1993), a publication of Christianity Today, Inc. Used by permission.

"Just Call Me Luci" taken from *You Bring the Confetti, God Brings the Joy* by Luci Swindoll. Copyright © 1986, Word Publishing, Nashville, Tennessee. All rights reserved..

"Was That a Sneeze?" taken from *Where There's Hope There's Laughter* by Hope Mihalap. Copyright © 1994, published by Knox Publishing and available from the author at 1316 Graydon Avenue, Norfolk, VA 23507, (757) 640-0333. Used by permission.

"A Hearty Ha, Ha, Ha!" by Barbara Johnson taken from *OverJoyed* by Patsy Clairmont, Barbara Johnson, Marilyn Meberg, Luci Swindoll, Sheila Walsh, and Thelma Wells. Copyright © 1999 by Women of Faith, Inc. Used by permission of Zondervan Publishing House.

"Telemarketers and Other Suppertime Annoyances" taken from *Chonda Pierce on Her Soapbox* by Chonda Pierce. Copyright © 1999 by Chonda Pierce. Used by permission of Zondervan Publishing House.

"Off in La-La Land" by Barbara Johnson taken from *We Brake for Joy!* by Patsy Clairmont, Barbara Johnson, Marilyn Meberg, Luci Swindoll,

Sheila Walsh, and Thelma Wells. Copyright © 1998 by Women of Faith, Inc. Used by permission of Zondervan Publishing House.

"Perfect Pitch?" taken from *Where There's Hope There's Laughter* by Hope Mihalap. Copyright © 1994, published by Knox Publishing and available from the author at 1316 Graydon Avenue, Norfolk, VA 23507, (757) 640-0333. Used by permission.

"I Know God Is Not a Grump Like Me" by Cynthia Yates is used by permission of the author.

"Teetering on the Verge of Wild Womandom" is taken from *A View from the Porch Swing* by Becky Freeman. Copyright © 1994, Broadman & Holman Publishers. All rights reserved. Used by permission.

"Snap Out of It!" taken from *Duh-Votions* by Sue Buchanan. Copyright © 1999 by Sue Buchanan. Used by permission of Zondervan Publishing House.

"Bad Mommy" by Marti Attoun. This article first appeared in *Christian Parenting* magazine (May/June 1994), a publication of Christianity Today, Inc. Used by permission.

"How to Obtain a Loan Using Your Children as Collateral" taken from *The Stomach Virus and Other Forms of Family Bonding* by Kathy Peel. Copyright © 1993, Word Publishing, Nashville, Tennessee. All rights reserved. Used by permission.

"Gung Ho!" by Marti Attoun. This article first appeared in *Christian Parenting* magazine (July/August 1992), a publication of Christianity Today, Inc. Used by permission.

"Private Parts" taken from *Just Hand Over the Chocolate and No One Will Get Hurt* by Karen Scalf Linamen. Copyright © 1999, published by Fleming H. Revell, a division of Baker Book House Company. Used by permission.

"Flex Time" by Marti Attoun. This article first appeared in *Christian Parenting* magazine (March/April 1993), a publication of Christianity Today, Inc. Used by permission.

"Suit Yourself" by Candace Walters. This article first appeared in *Today's Christian Woman* magazine (July/August 1992), a publication of Christianity Today. Inc. Used by permission.

"From the Mouths of Babes" pieces by Jeanne Michaud, Susan VanAllsburg, Beth Strong, M. L. Ackley, and Kim Biasotto first appeared in the following issues of *Christian Parenting* and *Christian Parenting Today*, a publication of Christianity Today, Inc.: (January/February 1993), (September/October 1991), (September/October 1991), (July/August

1997), (September/October 1998). Used by permission. Pieces by Wilette Wehner, Kirsten Jackson, and Gwen Scherling first appeared in the following issues of *Today's Christian Woman* magazine, a publication of Christianity Today, Inc.: (March/April 1999), (January/February 1995), (March/April 1999). Used by permission. Pieces by Clara Null, Sonja R. Ely, Donna Garrett, Michael Amedick, and Valerie A. Norris first appeared in the following issues of *Christian Reader*, a publication of Christianity Today, Inc.: (May/June 1999), (September/October 1996), (May/June 1999), (May/June 1999), (March/April 1999). Used by permission. The piece by Liz Curtis Higgs is taken from *Only Angels Can Wing It* (Nashville, TN: Thomas Nelson Publishers, 1995). Used by permission.

"Worms in My Tea" taken from *Worms in My Tea* by Becky Freeman. Copyright © 1994, Broadman & Holman Publishers. All rights reserved. Used by permission.

"How Will I Find You When I Get to Heaven?" by Ellie Lofaro is used by permission of the author.

"Pacified" taken from *Choosing the Amusing* by Marilyn Meberg. Copyright © 1999, Word Publishing, Nashville, Tennessee. All rights reserved. Used by permission.

"Scorched" taken from *Finding Gifts in Everyday Life* by Nancy Coey. Copyright © 1995 by Nancy Coey. Sweetwater Press, Raleigh, North Carolina. Used by permission.

"Who's the Boss?" reprinted from *Detours, Tow Trucks and Angels in Disguise* by Carol Kent. Copyright © 1996 by Carol Kent. Used by permission of NavPress, Colorado Springs, CO. All rights reserved. For copies call (800) 366-7788.

"The Art of Potty Training" taken from *The Stomach Virus and Other Forms of Family Bonding* by Kathy Peel. Copyright © 1993, Word Publishing, Nashville, Tennessee. All rights reserved. Used by permission.

"Body Snatchers" by Karen M. Leet. This article first appeared in *Christian Home and School* magazine (September 1991). Used by permission.

"Friendship Bread" by Liz Curtis Higgs taken from *Only Angels Can Wing It* (Nashville, TN: Thomas Nelson Publishers, 1995). Used by permission.

"Stormy Weather" by Thelma Wells used by permission of the author.

"Shades of Lucy and Ethel" is taken from *Alchemy of the Heart* by Luci Swindoll. Copyright © 1984. Used by permission.

"Wax Buildup, Anthropology, and Starched Pillowcases" by Sue Buchanan taken from *Friends through Thick and Thin* by Gloria Gaither, Peggy Benson, Sue Buchanan, Joy MacKenzie. Copyright © 1998 by Gloria Gaither, Peggy Benson, Sue Buchanan, Joy MacKenzie. Used by permission of Zondervan Publishing House.

"'Ssshhh! You're in Church!'" The first three pieces are taken from *Awkward Christian Soldiers* by Ken Alley. Copyright © 1998, Harold Shaw Publishers, Wheaton, IL. Used by permission. Piece by Sue Shoger first appeared in *Christian Reader* (January/February 1999), a publication of Christianity Today, Inc. Used by permission.

"Praise Ye the Lord!" taken from *Sportin' a Tude* by Patsy Clairmont, a Focus on the Family book published by Tyndale House. Copyright © 1996 by Patsy Clairmont. All rights reserved. International copyright secured. Used by permission.

"Your Chickens Will Come Home to Roost" by Susan Duke taken from *Courage for the Chicken-Hearted* by Becky Freeman, Susan Duke, Rebecca Barlow Jordan, Gracie Malone, and Fran Caffey Sandin. Copyright © 1998, Honor Books. Used by permission.

"Antics" taken from *Choosing the Amusing* by Marilyn Meberg. Copyright © 1999, Word Publishing, Nashville, Tennessee. All rights reserved. Used by permission.

"What Time Is It When the Chickadee Chicks?" taken from *Chonda Pierce on Her Soapbox* by Chonda Pierce. Copyright © 1999 by Chonda Pierce. Used by permission of Zondervan Publishing House.

"Hair Today ... Gone Tomorrow" by Sheila Walsh taken from *OverJoyed* by Patsy Clairmont, Barbara Johnson, Marilyn Meberg, Luci Swindoll, Sheila Walsh, and Thelma Wells. Copyright © 1999 by Women of Faith, Inc. Used by permission of Zondervan Publishing House.

"Find It at Your Local Bookstore" is taken from *Second Row Piano Side* by Chonda Pierce, copyright © 1996, Beacon Hill Press, Kansas City, MO. Used by permission.

"Tolerance" is taken from *Couldn't We Just Kill 'Em and Tell God They Died?* by Cathy Lechner (Lake Mary, FL: Creation House. Copyright © 1997, 121). Used by permission.

"Midlife Bliss" by Becky Freeman taken from *Courage for the Chicken-Hearted* by Becky Freeman, Susan Duke, Rebecca Barlow Jordan, Gracie Malone, and Fran Caffey Sandin. Copyright © 1998, Honor Books. Used by permission.

"Keep Your Tweezers to Yourself!" by Gracie Malone is taken from *Courage for the Chicken-Hearted* by Becky Freeman, Susan Duke,

Rebecca Barlow Jordan, Gracie Malone, and Fran Caffey Sandin, copyright © 1998, Honor Books. Used by permission.

"Love Those Wrinkles!" is taken from *Forty Reasons Why Life Is More Fun after the Big 4-0* (Nashville, TN: Thomas Nelson Publishers, 1997). Used by permission.

"Ho, Ho, No!" by Nancy Kennedy. This article was first published in *Marriage Partnership* magazine (Winter 1994), a publication of Christianity Today, Inc. Used by permission.

"Picture Perfect" by Marti Attoun. This article first appeared in *Christian Parenting* magazine (November/December 1990), a publication of Christianity Today, Inc. Used by permission.

"This Little Piggy Went to Day Care" taken from *A Funny Thing Happened on the Way to Heaven* by Connie Breedlove. Copyright © 1996 by Connie Macsas Breedlove. Used by permission of Zondervan Publishing House.

"I Love Cats!" taken from *Mom to Mom* by Elisa Morgan. Copyright © 1996 by Elisa Morgan. Used by permission of Zondervan Publishing House.

"All I Want for Christmas" taken from *The Twelve Dazes of Christmas* by Charlene Ann Baumbich. Copyright © 1996 by Charlene Ann Baumbich. Used with permission from InterVarsity Press, P.O. Box 1400, Downers Grove, IL 60515.

Women of Faith

Women of Faith is partnering with
Zondervan Publishing House, Integrity Music,
Today's Christian Woman magazine, World Vision,
Campus Crusade, International Bible Society, New
Life Ministries & New Life Clinics, Partnership
Clean Web.Net, and Crossings Book Club to offer
conferences, publications, worship music,
and inspirational gifts that support and
encourage today's Christian women.

Since their beginning in January of 1996,
Women of Faith conferences have
enjoyed an enthusiastic welcome
by women across the country.

**Call 1-888-49-FAITH for the many
conference locations and dates available.**

Resources for Women of Faith^{SM}

BOOKS

The Joyful Journey
Bring Back the Joy
Friends Through Thick and Thin
Joy Breaks
We Brake for Joy!
OverJoyed!
Outrageous Joy
Extravagant Grace

WOMEN OF FAITH BIBLE STUDIES SERIES

Celebrating Friendship
Discovering Your Spiritual Gifts
Embracing Forgiveness
Experiencing God's Presence
Finding Joy
Growing in Prayer
Knowing God's Will
Strengthening Your Faith

WOMEN OF FAITH WOMEN OF THE BIBLE BIBLE STUDY SERIES

Deborah: Daring to Be Different for God
Esther: Becoming a Woman God Can Use
Hannah: Entrusting Your Dreams to God
Mary: Choosing the Joy of Obedience
Ruth: Trusting That God Will Provide for You
Sarah: Facing Life's Uncertainties with a Faithful God

WOMEN OF FAITH ZONDERVANGROUPWARE^{TM}

Capture the Joy Kit
Capture the Joy Leader's Guide
Capture the Joy Participant's Guide

Other books by Ann Spangler:

Women of the Bible
A One-Year Devotional Study of Women in Scripture
Coauthored with Jean E. Syswerda
ISBN: 0-310-22352-0

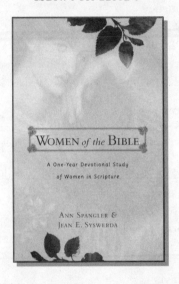

Let the Lives of Women of the Bible Touch Your Life Today

Women of the Bible focuses on fifty-two remarkable women in Scripture—women whose struggles to live with faith and courage are not unlike our own. Far from being cardboard characters, these women encourage us through their failures as well as their successes. You'll see how God acted in surprising and wonderful ways to draw them—and you—to himself. This year-long devotional offers a unique method to help you slow down and savor the story of God's unrelenting love for his people, offering a fresh perspective that will nourish and strengthen your personal communion with him.

Dreams and Miracles
How God Speaks Through Your Dreams
ISBN: 0-310-22907-3

A Miracle a Day
Stories of Heavenly Encounters
Hardcover ISBN: 0-310-20794-0

An Angel a Day
Stories of Angelic Encounters
ISBN: 0-310-48720-X

We want to hear from you. Please send your comments about this book to us in care of the address below. Thank you.

ZondervanPublishingHouse
Grand Rapids, Michigan 49530
http://www.zondervan.com